BOEING
WIDEBODIES

M I C H A E L   H A E N G G I

MBI

DEDICATION

Dad, this "two" is for you.

First published in 2003 by Motorbooks International, Galtier Plaza, Suite 200, 380 Jackson Street, St. Paul, MN 55101-3885 USA

© Mike Haenggi, 2003

The information in this book is true and complete to the best of our knowledge. All recommendations are made without any guarantee on the part of the author or Publisher, who also disclaim any liability incurred in connection with the use of this data or specific details.

We recognize that some words, model names and designations, for example, mentioned herein are the property of the trademark holder. We use them for identification purposes only. This is not an official publication.

Motorbooks International titles are also available at discounts in bulk quantity for industrial or sales-promotional use. For details write to Special Sales Manager at Motorbooks International Wholesalers & Distributors, Galtier Plaza, Suite 200, 380 Jackson Street, St. Paul, MN 55101-3885 USA

ISBN 0-7603-0842-X

On the front cover: Currently, the fastest conventional airliners cruise at Mach 0.85. The Sonic Cruiser is a new airliner concept designed to travel just under the speed of sound, with a cruise speed between Mach 0.95 and Mach 0.98.

On the frontispiece: Firewall the throttles on a Boeing 747-400, and you'll unleash 225,000 pounds of thrust from the plane's four engines. Typically all four throttles are used simultaneously, but they can be opened or closed individually if necessary.

On the title page: Two Northwest Airlines 747-200s at Minneapolis-St. Paul International Airport are parked for the night beneath the Minneapolis skyline. Northwest's headquarters and one of its biggest hubs are located here, so it's no surprise the company dominates the airport.

On the back cover, left: An all-new digital flight deck is one of the features that distinguishes a 747-400 from earlier models. Gone are most of the 747-20's analogous gauges, nearly two-thirds of its switches, and its flight engineer's station.

Edited by Steve Gansen
Designed by Brenda Canales

Printed in China

CONTENTS

ACKNOWLEDGMENTS

Creating even a small book such as this is impossible without the help of others. I offer my sincere thanks to my wife Michelle and daughter Samara. Their hard work allowed me to make this book happen. I give thanks to my other family members who chipped in too, including Barbara Haenggi; Jeff, Jamie, and Gillian Haenggi; and Terry and Bev Dunnigan. My appreciation also goes to Tom Aniello and the crew at Pilatus Business Aircraft for their support as well as to Notis Pagiavlas, Ph.D., of Embry-Riddle Aeronautical University for his guidance.

My hat is off to the marvelous employees at the Boeing Company, including Mary E. Kane, Tom Lubbesmeyer, and Barbara Bird, for their help with photography and archival images. The special access given by Liz Harrison and Harry Beatty of Northwest Airlines was outstanding and much appreciated. Thanks to Jim Stump of General Electric Aircraft Engines for supplying some beautiful product shots and to Ralph Olson of *Airliners* magazine for allowing me access to his extensive archives. I'm also grateful to authors Guy Norris and Mark Wagner. Their excellent airliner books are a must for any enthusiast.

And finally, my sincere appreciation goes to the folks at MBI Publishing Company, including Steve Gansen, Lee Klancher, Zack Miller, Becky Pagel, Carol Weiss, Sara Perfetti, and Amy Glaser. I'm grateful for their nearly endless patience with me as I wrote this book.

A Colorado sky reflects off the fuselage of this United 747-400 as it taxis to its gate at Denver International Airport on a sunny afternoon. Soon it will load 400 passengers and all their bags, several tons of freight, and 55,000 gallons of fuel and head overseas on a nonstop flight.

INTRODUCTION

As the world's first widebody airliner, the Boeing 747 has earned a permanent place among man's greatest inventions. "Boeing airplanes change the world, bringing people, ideas, and opportunity together, increasing global understanding and prosperity," said Alan Mulally, Boeing Commercial Airplanes Group president. "The 747 is at the heart of this legacy."

The significance of the 747 is hard to overstate. The New York Museum of Modern Art recently added the 747 to the list of items desired for its design collection. "The 747 is beautiful," remarked the museum's curator, "because of how it looks, how it works, and what it represents." In November 1999, the 747 was immortalized on a U.S. postage stamp. It was showcased along with the Wright brothers' first flight and Lindbergh's crossing of the Atlantic as one of the top three aviation achievements of the twentieth century. "I think that's pretty good company," said Phil Condit, Boeing's chairman and chief executive officer.

The next time you're at the airport, take a moment to closely examine a 747 parked at a gate. You'll find it hard not to be amazed. A modern 747 is more than 230 feet long and six stories high. Fully loaded, it weighs 400,000 pounds. Despite its proportions, the 747 can blast down the runway, accelerate to more than 130 miles per hour, rotate, climb to an altitude of 40,000 feet, and then cruise for 8,000 miles. At its cruising altitude, the airliner can travel more than 600 miles per hour through air so cold and thin humans would be unable to breathe it. Of course, the 747 allows occupants to travel in pressurized, heated comfort. The airliner's navigation and communication systems direct it from city to city, day or night, rain or shine. After getting travelers safely to their destinations, the 747 accepts another group of passengers and repeats the process. People often take the widebody airliner for granted because Boeing created an incredible machine that has made such flights routine.

At the time the company launched the 747, Boeing had been building aircraft for more than 50 years. Many of the 747's predecessors were enduring symbols of their own eras. In the late 1930s, Boeing's 314 "Clipper" fostered trade and enabled opulent trips to the Far East. During World War II, Boeing's B-17 and B-29 became icons of American military might. Boeing again took the world by storm in 1954 when it introduced its first jet airliner, the 707, and began a dynasty that continues today. Boeing had successfully built hundreds of aircraft types before creating the pivotal 747, the biggest jetliner the world had ever seen.

That first widebody became a springboard off which Boeing launched an entire line of giant aircraft. The 747 eventually spawned 13 commercial variants, extending its life well into the twenty-first century. A decade after the 747 first flew, Boeing introduced its next widebody airliner, an advanced medium twin called the 767. The 767 prompted six variants and became the dominant airliner flying the world's transatlantic routes. With the 747 and the 767, Boeing had revolutionized the airliner industry twice. When the company flew the 777 for the first time in 1994, it did it again. The 777 took the widebody twin-engine concept to new performance heights and completely changed the way Boeing built aircraft.

The 777 spawned five additional variants, bringing the total widebody lineup to 23 models. And if Boeing's advanced studies on the drawing board today give us any hint to the future, we will soon see a new widebody rewriting the rules of air travel once again.

Traveling 600 miles per hour at an altitude of 40,000 feet is now so routine, many passengers fall asleep in flight. Most are unaware of the incredible journey Boeing accomplished to design and build the airplane around them.

chapter 1

747
Heart of the Legacy

Boeing's 747 prototype rolled out of the company's hangar in Everett, Washington, and into public view for the first time on September 30, 1968. The world was stunned at its size. The 747 dwarfed every airliner in the skies. When compared to the 707-320, Boeing's biggest airliner at the time, the 747 was 80 feet longer, 20 feet taller, had a wingspan 50 feet wider, and carried twice as many passengers. The aviation media, searching for an adequate way to describe the massive airliner, coined the term "jumbo jet." And the 747 was the centerpiece of a jumbo celebration. The rollout ceremony represented the culmination of six years of work by tens of thousands of Boeing employees and contractors. For a few minutes at least, all of them stood in appreciation of the spectacle they had created. However, most knew the celebration would be short lived. There was still an enormous amount of work ahead in order to flight-test the aircraft and prove its design. The stakes riding on the success of the program could not have been any higher. If the 747 failed, Boeing would likely go bankrupt, and most people at the celebration would be out of a job. In many ways, it was a wonder the company had even gotten to this point.

The roots of the 747 program date back to 1962, during the height of the Cold War. The U.S. military

On September 30, 1968, Boeing unveiled the 747 to the public. As a salute to its potential customers, the aircraft carried the insignia of 28 airlines from around the world on its forward fuselage. *Boeing*

Supersonic airliners were predicted to be the next greatest thing when Boeing's designers conceived the 747. Due to their expense and extraordinary operating costs, ultimately only two types of supersonic aircraft were ever built—the Tupolev Tu-144 and the Concorde (pictured).

needed aircraft that could ferry massive numbers of American soldiers and equipment across the Atlantic Ocean to Europe in the event of a Soviet invasion. The federal government put out a contract for a mammoth new military airlifter dubbed the CX-HLS. Boeing, Douglas, and Lockheed all competed to build it. The proposed aircraft was so big that no engine in production at that time was powerful enough to lift it off the ground. New technology high-bypass turbofans were developed to offer double the thrust of conventional jet engines of the day. These new engines were essential both to the birth of the airlifter and to the 747. As Boeing developed its airlifter proposal, it simultaneously started toying around with the idea of a giant civilian airliner that could take advantage of the powerful new engines.

Lockheed created the C-5 Galaxy and eventually won the CX-HLS contract in 1965 by underbidding Boeing and Douglas. Boeing's designers were disappointed about losing the $250 million contract but were pleased to have generated some significant ideas for a new airliner that was larger than anything else flying. The day after Boeing lost the CX-HLS contract, Joe Sutter, one of the company's chief designers, gathered together about 100 engineers and began making drawings of airliners that could take advantage of the new high-bypass-ratio engines. Because the engineers did not know what size to make the airplane, they sketched out three different prototypes: a 250-seater, a 300-seater, and a 350-seater. They took the drawings to some of the major airlines at the time, including Pan American Airlines, Japan Air Lines,

The 747 was designed from the start to haul freight. Looking down the unobstructed length of the airliner through its nose cargo door, you can see why having a raised cockpit was beneficial for straight-in cargo loading. *Boeing*

Lufthansa, and British Overseas Airways Corporation. The engineers asked for feedback and were shocked to find out that many airlines wanted an airliner more than double the size of the 120-seat 707, Boeing's largest product at the time. Armed with a new understanding of airline preferences, they returned to Seattle to ponder the implications of building a massive jetliner.

The 747 had a long road ahead before it would become anything more than a design study. The competition the embryonic 747 faced was both internal and external. It was forced to fight other Boeing projects for already allocated resources and had to battle other manufacturers' airplanes for success in the marketplace. At the time of the CX-HLS award in 1965, Boeing's commercial jet aircraft production lines were already in full swing on other models. The 707 had been in production for several years in its -120, -138, -320, and -420 incarnations. The similar 720 and 720B also were moving down the lines. These four-engine narrowbodies were the largest commercial aircraft rolling out of Boeing's factory at the time. Just two years earlier, the company had unveiled its short-haul 727-100. Meanwhile, the 737-100 and 737-200 were in the advanced stages of design and only a few years away from their first flights. The jetliner business was booming, a fact not overlooked by Boeing's competitors, certainly not by its chief rival, Douglas.

With its DC-8, Douglas had been competing toe-to-toe with Boeing's 707 for more than five years. In its next phase of one-upmanship, Douglas was aiming

Manufacturing a 747 is no small affair. Here Boeing prepares to move the forward fuselage back to join the wing and center section. This photo was taken June 22, 1968, in an era of much less automation than we know today. *Boeing*

to deal another blow to Boeing's flagship by offering the DC-8 in the stretched -60 and -70 series. Douglas's management had already started marketing the stretched versions to the airlines, touting their significant size-advantage over the 707. Douglas was also looking to capture more of the domestic market by building the earliest versions of the short-haul DC-9 in the -10, -30, and -40 configurations. Like their counterparts at Boeing, Douglas engineers were also eager to capitalize on the new high-bypass turbofans developed for the CX-HLS contract. In 1968, American Airlines expressed desire for a new high-capacity, medium-haul, widebody airliner. Douglas was quick to answer, and the DC-10 was penned onto the drawing board.

Boeing and Douglas were not the only manufacturers with plans to capture airliner market share

in the latter part of the 1960s. Just down the street at its plant in Burbank, Lockheed was also attempting to cash in on the American Airlines contract by designing its own high-capacity, medium-haul, widebody trijet. Lockheed's version was the 250-seat L-1011.

Meanwhile, across the Atlantic, a new pan-European entity had just formed to build a medium-range widebody specifically for the European market. It would later become the Airbus A300.

Like the 747, all the widebodies were just ideas at the time. But Boeing knew it was potentially facing competition on all fronts. The 747 project was further complicated by the industry's fervor over supersonic airliners. The military had been flying supersonic fighters for years, and now airframe manufacturers were buzzing with the idea of building supersonic airliners, also called

Taking center stage under a sea of factory lights, the third 747 ever built is readied for rollout in the spring of 1969. From here it will be hauled to the paint shop to receive its airline paint scheme. *Boeing*

13

supersonic transports or SSTs. Analysts forecasted it was not a question of if the faster aircraft would be built but rather when and by whom.

In the late 1960s, the public was caught up in the space race. Project Apollo was in full swing, and the jet- and rocket-powered craze was sweeping the world. The race to the moon would soon culminate with the *Eagle* landing on the Sea of Tranquillity. Capitalizing on the public's fascination with new technologies, aircraft manufacturers and airlines labored to showcase their futuristic capabilities, and many believed supersonic airliners were the answer. The SST movement was so prevalent that each airframer was considering building one. At an International Air Transport Association in 1967, forecasts predicted a market for 1,250 SSTs between 1972 and 1978. Many experts in the aerospace

Using platforms that hang down from the ceiling, Boeing workers prep a 747 for its next coat of paint. On average, it takes 300 gallons to cover a 747. The paint adds 1,200 pounds of weight to the aircraft. *Boeing*

The first 747 took its maiden flight on February 9, 1969. Shadowed by a Boeing-owned F-86 chase plane, the 747 reached a speed of 280 miles per hour and an altitude of 15,000 feet. In his post-flight briefing, project pilot Jack Waddell lauded the plane's performance. *Boeing*

industry believed SSTs would render subsonic jetliners obsolete, relegating them to hauling cargo. It was this belief that caused the SST program to have a profound effect on the development of the 747. Despite its groundbreaking size, the 747 was designed to haul freight. Boeing assumed its SST concept, a Mach 2.7 250-passenger airliner dubbed the 2707, would become the company's flagship model.

Back in 1964, forecasts had predicted that world passenger traffic would grow 12 percent per year for 10 years, while cargo would grow 22 percent per year over the same period. This rate of growth translated into a need for 346 more 747s, 242 more passenger models, and 60 more freighters by 1974. Even in a supersonic world, Boeing's analysis showed a ready market for the 747.

The government-sponsored research on large airplanes from the CX-HLS contract and a forecast of positive competitive and economic conditions fortified Boeing's commitment to the 747 project despite the adversarial forces. Aggressive maneuvering from Pan Am in 1965 helped push Boeing over the edge.

"You either need to propose a bigger airplane, or we're going to buy stretch DC-8s and your 707 line is going to hurt pretty bad," said Juan Trippe, president of Pan Am, to the Boeing 747's chief engineer, Joe Sutter. For an airframer, a request for a new product rarely gets any clearer.

The simplest and most cost-effective way for Boeing to deliver a larger aircraft to an airline was to stretch the 707. Boeing's initial interest in this option was acknowledged informally at the end of May 1964. Two versions of the 707 Stretch, the intercontinental 707-820 and the domestic 707-620, were floated to the airlines in early 1965. Both were versions of the basic 707-320, upgraded with extended fuselages, larger wings, and more powerful engines. After further design work, engineers discovered that the bigger wing and longer fuselage required an extensive redesign of the main undercarriage and wing carry-through structure.

A modern desktop computer probably has more power than all of this equipment combined, but this technology was vital for monitoring flight parameters in 1969. Here an engineer makes final wiring checks aboard the 747 prior to another sortie. *Boeing*

Water tanks provided ballast to simulate passenger and cargo loads for flight testing. Not only could the tanks simulate various amounts of weight, they could also shift the weight fore and aft in flight through connecting pipes to test different center-of-gravity configurations. *Boeing*

After a long flight from Paris, an Air France 747-200 taxis to its gate at Miami International Airport. All of Air France's 747-200s are powered by General Electric CF6-50E2s.

The 747SP was the hot rod of the 747 fleet, able to fly farther, higher, and faster than the rest of the variants. A shortened fuselage, taller tail, and lightened structure helped a 747SP set a world record on a nonstop delivery flight from Paine Field, Washington, to Cape Town, South Africa—a distance of 8,940 nautical miles. *Boeing*

To ensure the longer model would have proper clearance to rotate and take off, it needed longer landing gear. This, in turn, necessitated larger bays into which to retract the gear. Sutter recalled, "Boeing people decided that spending money on the 707 wasn't worth it because it would be a lot of money, and the program would not last very long." The Douglas DC-8, on the other hand, was successfully stretched to make the -61 series, thanks primarily to its longer-legged landing gear. It offered greater capacity without significant expense.

Forced back to the drawing board at the beginning of 1966, Boeing's design group opted for a completely new airliner, one dubbed the 747. Starting with a clean sheet, Boeing was free to make the new aircraft as large as modern technology would allow. It was designed around four of the giant new turbofans developed during competition for the CX-HLS contract. The first proposals looked nothing like the 747s we see today. In the cross section, the aircraft had a "double bubble" two-deck fuselage based on the 707 that looked somewhat like a figure eight in cross section. Its variants, the -3, -4, and -5, each had a different length and wing size to offer a variety of passenger capacity and range configurations. The problem was that airlines didn't like the idea of a double-decker aircraft, citing loading and servicing problems as well as concerns about the ability to safely evacuate passengers from the upper decks. Should passengers have had to evacuate the upper deck in an emergency, their drop down a nearly vertical inflatable slide would have been approximately three stories.

With the SST program influencing the general mindset, Boeing modified the 747 design into one that was optimized for cargo. A new international standard for freight containers stated that, while they could vary in length up to 40 feet, their cross sections should be no more than eight feet wide and eight feet long. With that decree, Boeing knew exactly what its new 747 had to carry. After looking at the container problem, the

Inside a Northwest hangar, a 747–200 shows off its number two Pratt & Whitney JT9D. Northwest has historically favored putting Pratt engines on its aircraft. All of its 747–200s are equipped with JT9Ds, while the later -400 series is powered by the PW4056.

Here's what the inside wall of a 747 looks like without the interior installed. Clearly visible are the riveted fuselage ribs, window support structure, and rolls of insulation on the floor. The quick-connects for the passenger lights, vents, and attendant-call buttons can be seen hanging down.

Passengers wait at Amsterdam's Schiphol airport for their Taiwan-bound flight. Eva Air, part of the Evergreen Group, is a Taiwan-based airline that operates a fleet of ten 747-400s fitted with side cargo doors.

The 747's 16-wheel main landing gear is more than just posts and wheels. The plane has an oleo-pneumatic leveling system connected to suspension dampers to ensure that weight is spread evenly. Anti-lock brakes are standard, the body gear turns whenever the nose gear is turned past 20 degrees, and of course, it all neatly retracts after takeoff.

Top: The 747-400's automated flight deck greatly simplified cockpit procedures and checklists. The new cockpit has 34 items for normal procedures versus the 107 found in the old cockpit. The checklists can be called up on a digital screen if needed.

Bottom: A pilot flying a 747-400 has the most-needed information displayed on the two closest screens. On the left is the primary flight display, showing speed, altitude, heading, and attitude. This one shows the plane moving at 30 knots at an altitude of 920 feet above sea level (it is on the ground) on a heading of 299 degrees. On the right is the navigation display showing heading, a compass arc, and some of the navigation frequencies in use.

Two scissor-lift catering trucks service the *City of Freetown*, a KLM 747-400. The Dutch airline operates a fleet of CF6-powered 747s, which fly from Amsterdam to destinations in Australia, Asia, Africa, and the United States.

Boeing team quickly realized the 747 would be most efficient if it could carry two rows of containers side by side and be able to load long containers straight in through the nose or tail. It was this realization that resulted in today's widebody jet. Further cargo studies proved loading through the nose was preferred over loading through the tail. This dictated a hinged nose section and a cockpit raised above the cargo deck to keep it out of the way. When designers made the raised cockpit aerodynamic with the rest of the fuselage, they created the trademark "hump" of the 747 design.

Boeing's path to the final configuration of the 747 was indeed circuitous. Engineers labored over the 747 design to ensure that it could evolve gracefully from the premier passenger jetliner into a freighter as soon as SSTs started passing it in the skies. Boeing was ready, and customers were already lining up at the doors.

PROGRAM LAUNCH

The 747 reached formal project status in March 1966. Just a month later, Boeing had a $500 million order for 25 aircraft from Pan Am. Boeing also held letters of intent from Japan Airlines and Lufthansa and a "strong commitment" to buy from Trans World Airlines, Air France, BOAC, and Continental Airlines. Boeing had both hard and soft orders in hand, but before it could

This Singapore Airlines 747-400, registered 9V-SPK, was completely destroyed in a crash on takeoff at Chiang Kai Shek Airport in Taipei on October 31, 2000. Hampered by an approaching typhoon and limited visibility, the pilots mistook a closed runway for the active one and attempted to take off. The runway they picked was under construction. The plane accelerated to takeoff speed before it hit cement barricades and construction vehicles parked on the runway. There were 83 fatalities out of 179 on board. *AJ Smith, Flying Images Worldwide*

confirm a launch decision, the company needed to calculate the development costs.

Boeing estimated that it would cost $500 million for pre-production costs, including detailed engineering design, assembly line tooling, and initial material stocks. This money would also fund the incredible task of building a factory. Boeing figured another $500 million would be needed for labor and materials, advanced component and subassembly production, initial final assembly line activity, and the year-long flight test development program that would lead up to certification and first deliveries. All told, Boeing was looking at a bill of at least $1 billion to launch the 747 in 1966.

In order to manage this seemingly impossible sum, Boeing sought to share its risks by asking partner suppliers to take a piece of the capital risk pro-portional to the amount of revenues they might earn on the project. Because of this complex task, Boeing arranged a break-clause in its contract with Pan Am. The plan would enable the company to pull out of the program altogether with only minimal penalties if it decided the risk was too great. By subcontracting out just over 50 percent of the work in terms of dollars, Boeing was able to spread the risk around enough to make the deal easier to swallow. Approximately 1,500 prime suppliers and 15,000 secondary suppliers from 47 states and 6 countries provided parts and equipment for the new 747. Ultimately, it took Boeing three months to complete all the necessary supplier negotiations and to develop the site where it could actually build the aircraft. The numbers finally convinced Boeing that a market really existed for a giant subsonic jetliner.

The 747's long gestation came to an end when the first one rolled out of the factory and entered flight testing. Project pilot Jack Waddell and his test crew started with taxi tests, progressively increasing speed to ensure proper operation of the steering, brakes, flight controls, and thrust reversers. In the highest-speed taxi tests, the 747 reached 160 miles per hour. On February 9, 1969, Waddell and crew took the aircraft on its first flight. The 747 flew for about a half hour before suffering a minor malfunction of the flaps, forcing the crew to bring it back for a precautionary landing. When Waddell deplaned, he said, "It is ridiculously easy to fly; it almost lands itself."

Boeing quickly resolved the flap problem as news about the successful flight spread. More problems were found as testing continued, but none was insurmountable. Within five months of program launch, Boeing received $1.8 billion in orders for the 747, resulting in one of the largest backlogs of preproduction orders in commercial airplane history. Boeing's enormous risk paid off, and the program grew quickly. But even with this success, the company could not afford to rest on its laurels.

DERIVATIVES FOR LONGEVITY

Boeing gambled on the 747-100 and eventually won 250 orders for the new jetliner, but the story did not end there. The derivative models spawned from the original 747 contributed to Boeing's rise in prominence and ultimate success. Using the 747-100 as a base, Boeing leveraged its original investment in engineering and tooling and developed new models that could generate additional sales. The 747-100 spawned more than a dozen variants, including the 747-200, -300, -400, -400D, and -400ER, with many offered in passenger, passenger/freighter combination, pure freighter, and convertible configurations. As the original 747 design was repeatedly upgraded and improved to meet increasing customer demands, it continued to bring in more orders.

Model Series	No. of Customers	Total Orders	Total Deliveries
747 Orders and Deliveries Summary by Model			
747-100	32	250	250
747-200	59	393	393
747-300	19	81	81
747-400	35	453	431
747-400D	2	19	19
747-400ER	1	6	3
747-400ERF	4	11	3
747-400F	13	97	78
747-400M	13	61	61
Totals	86*	1371	1319

D = Domestic,   F = Freighter,   * Individual customers
ER=Extended Range,   M = Combination

Cumulative through December 2002   Source: Boeing

The contribution of the derivative models to the success of the 747 program cannot be understated. Of the 1,300-plus orders for the 747 series, only 250 of them were for the original 747-100 model.

Thirty-five years after the 747 program began, Boeing was still researching additional derivatives to determine if any could offer increased performance. In 2000, the 747X and 747X Stretch were on the drawing board, and Boeing shopped the marketplace to gauge airline interest. These versions, seating 430 and 520 passengers respectively, were heavily updated and lengthened versions of the 416-seat 747-400. The new models, dubbed "Next Generation 747s," relied on the original 747 design, but had advanced cockpits, high-technology wing designs new powerplants, and modern interiors. Boeing planned on offering the aircraft to provide direct competition to the 550-seat Airbus A380. Airbus allocated $12 billion for the development of the A380 program. Boeing, since it could fall back on previous work, was able to develop its 747-derived aircraft for around $4 billion. By stretching the 747, Boeing could compete in the same market as the A380 for one-third the development cost. Unfortunately for Boeing, airlines showed little interest at the time. As a result, the company shelved the giant 747s for further study.

Airlines reported that they didn't necessarily need

In terms of number of aircraft, the largest 747 operator in the world is the U.S. cargo airline Atlas Air. Here one of Atlas's 747-200s receives some evening maintenance. Note the side cargo door is open, and the flaps and slats on the wing are extended.

a bigger 747. Their main complaint was noise, as the 747 wasn't keeping up with the tightening noise restrictions, especially those at London Heathrow Airport. Among major airport hubs, Heathrow had, and continues to have, some of the lowest thresholds for jet noise in the world. If an aircraft cannot keep noise below a certain decibel level, it is subject to a curfew. This means that noisy aircraft cannot use Heathrow during curfew hours. If an aircraft is en route when the curfew is in effect, it must divert and land somewhere else. If the plane is at an airport during restricted curfew hours, it must wait until morning to depart. Logically, airlines do their best to avoid either situation.

In 2002, Boeing unveiled its solution to this problem, presenting a new concept dubbed the 747-400X QLR. The "X" in the title signified it as a variation of the 747-400 model. QLR was the abbreviation for Quiet Longer Range. In order to make the new 747 more environmentally friendly, the engines were given new acoustic liners and were equipped with "chevron"-shaped cowlings around the fan and core exhausts. The result was a 20 percent reduction in what is known as "noise area level" on takeoff and a decrease of 40 percent on landing compared to the levels of a standard 747-400.

With these improvements, the 747-400X QLR could operate comfortably within Heathrow's QC2 curfew limits. Further improvements on the plane included extra fuel storage in the horizontal tail tank and a gross weight increase from 910,000 pounds to 921,000 pounds. Rather than the standard 747-400 winglets, the QLR sported raked wingtips similar to those found on the extended-range 777 and the 767-400ER. Other improved wing features included new ailerons, new outboard flaps, and a trailing-edge wedge adapted from the MD-11. With these enhancements, the jetliner's range increased to 7,980 nautical miles, 310 miles farther than the standard 747-400.

With deliveries of 747s continuing to this day, Boeing hopes the QLR will be the next variant to help carry the 747 line well into the future. Its nearly four decades of production makes the 747 Boeing's longest running commercial program. Over 1,300 aircraft have rolled off Boeing's production line, and analysts estimate that the models have brought in more than $130 billion in sales. Remembering that the original 747 gamble involved roughly a $1 billion investment for program launch, it's easy to get a sense of the value of the 747 to Boeing.

chapter 2

767
Transatlantic Titan

As the 1960s gave way to the 1970s, Boeing grew increasingly restless for a new product. Salespeople were clamoring for a new airplane and didn't even seem to care what it was as long as it was new. There was also concern among Boeing's board of directors that the firm's next generation of leaders was not being trained in the best way possible—by developing a new plane of their own.

Fortunately, before the urgency for a new product came to the forefront, Boeing had quietly worked on a couple of key studies that helped pave the way for what was to come. In 1969, Boeing assembled the New Airplane Program study group to review past experiences with each of its major jet airliner programs. The group examined the lessons learned during the creation of the 707, 727, 737, and 747 in hopes that past problems would not be repeated and successful practices could be continued. The process, known as "Project Homework," took three years and produced a long list of ideas and as well as a new way to estimate development costs of future airliner programs.

At Boeing's narrowbody facility at Renton, another study was underway. Swissair, the national airline of Switzerland, was looking for a high-capacity,

American Airlines was one of the first airlines to order the 767. The airline ultimately owned one of the largest fleets of the type by taking delivery of twenty-nine 767-200s and sixty-seven 767-300s. All of American's 767s were powered by the GE CF6. *Boeing*

Boeing launched the 767 and 757 in tandem as companion high-technology twins. The aircraft are completely different configurations, but they share a common two-crew flight deck and systems. Even though the 767 is a much larger carrier than the 757, the operation of the two is so similar that pilots qualified to fly one are automatically qualified on the other. *Boeing*

short- to medium-haul airliner to use on its European trunk routes, the airways that connect major cities. Boeing thought it could meet this need with a twin-aisle version of the 727, dubbed the 727XX, and built a mockup to show Swissair.

After a lengthy decision-making process, Swissair ended up rejecting the 727XX and buying the Airbus A310 instead. Even in defeat, Boeing still liked its mockup, which was essentially the nose section of a 727 grafted onto a bulging fuselage measuring around 16 feet in diameter. Boeing continued studying high-capacity, medium-range aircraft. Attempting to find a compromise, it considered the idea of a "semi-widebody" design, a model offering a width somewhere between that of the 707 and the 747.

In 1972, Boeing chairman T. A. Wilson launched a new airplane study, calling it the 7X7. Its goal was

very broad—to define and develop Boeing's next airplane. Boeing decided right from the start to enter into an equal partnership with Aeritalia. The Italian aircraft firm was looking for an advanced STOL, short-range airliner dubbed QSH (quiet short haul). The deal was a departure for Boeing in that it was the company's first major international development program. Since the QSH project shared many goals with the 7X7, Boeing saw the deal as a way to spread out the huge costs of development, which could no longer be supported by a single company. Boeing also hoped the plan would result in sales to its partner's national and regional marketplace.

For the same reasons, Boeing also entered into a joint venture with Japan. The country was studying a short-range, 150-seat jet called the YX. The YX program was short-lived and was gradually absorbed into the larger 7X7 program. This enabled Japan's Civil Transport Development Corporation, or CTDC, to get involved with bigger aircraft.

Back in Italy, the QSH program soon found itself losing favor among airlines because the proposed model was too small. Everyone wanted a larger jet, so Boeing presented more variations with greater range and capacity. The 7X7 was slowly evolving into an airliner with transcontinental range. As the 7X7 concept grew in size, Aeritalia's interest waned, and subsequently the Italian share in the project dropped from 50 to 20 percent. Based on its extensive discussions with airlines all over the world, Boeing believed that it was moving in the right direction. Still, the airliner's final configuration remained highly uncertain. Compounding this was an Arab oil embargo, which resulted in an unstable market for airliners.

In 1973, Boeing consolidated the available market information and came up with two variants that best matched airline needs. The first was a medium-range twin with under-wing engines, the second a long-range trijet with two under-wing engines and a third mounted in the tail. Though these designs moved another step toward the reality of a larger jetliner, neither Boeing nor the airlines were quite satisfied with the size. Boeing had to soldier on with more 7X7 research.

DELAYS LEAD TO WINDFALLS

Boeing contacted more than 25 airlines for input during the years 1974 and 1975, representing the firm's first tentative steps toward embracing full customer involvement in its new product development process. Boeing found that the airlines' two major concerns were fuel efficiency and noise. The 7X7 project development

The prototype 767-200, displaying company colors, climbs out of Boeing field on a summer day in 1982. The narrowest widebody in service, the 767 first flew on September 26, 1981, and entered service twelve months later. *Boeing*

During flight testing, Boeing engineers streamed red and blue paint on the planes' engine pylons and wing-to-body fairing to help them better visualize airflow over the surfaces. Clean aerodynamics are crucial for an airliner to maximize speed and range by minimizing drag and fuel burn. *Boeing*

delays luckily coincided with major advances that addressed both of the airlines' concerns. Breakthroughs in airfoil and engine technology offered significant gains in both fuel efficiency and noise. An advanced wing design utilizing aft-loaded supercritical aerodynamics allowed for precise control of airflow over the wings and offered significant savings in fuel burn. In addition, General Electric and Pratt & Whitney introduced new technology engines that cut down on noise.

To determine the best configuration to capitalize on these breakthroughs, Boeing studied more than 100 different designs in the wind tunnel. Boeing again studied all the market data and refined it down to two vari-

ants. The company presented its new designs to the public for the first time at the 1975 Paris Air Show. One was a 200-seat model for the U.S. domestic market, the other a 175-seater for use in Europe. Both were configured as trijets with the option of either conventional or high t-tails.

The 7X7 body was designed to cater to the "people market rather than the freighter market," said Jack Steiner, vice president and general manager of narrowbody aircraft. The fuselage width, one of the most critical components when determining airliner configuration, was based on the optimal seat configuration across the cabin. Airlines liked five or six

The 767 assembly line is a maze of platforms and stairs. Once work is finished, all scaffolding is rolled out of the way so that the aircraft can be moved to the next station in the assembly line. On several of its production lines, Boeing is replacing this process with a new one that uses giant moving assembly lines like those used in the auto manufacturing business. *Boeing*

seats abreast in first class, seven in economy, and eight for high-density charter operations, ideally resulting in a 198-inch cross section. The cross section, about two-thirds the size of that on other widebody trijets, was great for fitting passenger seats. However, it was unable to carry two standard freight containers side by side in the cargo hold, a feature that drove the design width of the 747. Boeing pressed on, wagering that smaller, custom-made containers would be widely adopted to compensate for this drawback. Demand failed to materialize in 1975, and the 7X7 study carried over to 1976.

The width issue was decided, but discussions about whether the aircraft should be a trijet

The passenger compartment is only the top half of an airliner. The lower cargo deck of even a small widebody like the 767 is large enough to hold a compact car. Cargo bays are pressurized and temperature-controlled just like the main cabin. *Boeing*

continued. One school of thought, led by United Airlines, favored three engines for the extra performance needed in the "hot and high" conditions found at high-elevation airports like Denver International Airport. The other approach, endorsed by Western Airlines and Delta Air Lines, wanted the better economy that came with twin-engine aircraft. Since airliners often operate ten to fifteen hours per day, year after year, a few dollars per hour less in operating costs quickly adds up to millions of dollars in savings for the airline.

After a harsh debate among senior management at Boeing, the fuel-efficient twin ultimately won out and

was given top priority. But even after the decision was made, the trijet remained on the table as an option. In February 1978, Boeing added the 767 to its family of airliners and offered three options. The 767-100 was a 180- to 190-seat, medium-range twin. The larger 767-200 was also designed for medium range and seated up to 210. The trijet version, designated the 767MR/LR, was a 200-seater with intercontinental range.

PROGRAM LAUNCH

Presented with the 767's final configuration, Boeing's board of directors was finally asked to commit to launching the project. The company had already spent

Some days, working on a new airliner is just plain fun. Here a 767's escape slide is tested to ensure passengers can exit the plane quickly in the event of an emergency. Although it may seem frivolous, the tests are taken very seriously. Escape slides are a key safety feature of all widebody airliners. *Boeing*

$100 million developing the airliner, but up to that point, all expenditures were regarded as research and development. The time had come for Boeing to either start incurring up-front costs of several billion dollars or delay the project yet again. The board agreed to launch the new plane, but only if two conditions were met. It required that at least one foreign and two domestic airlines make commitments to purchase, and it asked that preproduction orders total at least 100 planes.

On July 14, 1978, some twelve years after 7X7 studies commenced, Boeing got its first customer for the 767 when United placed a $1 billion order for thirty 767-200s. By November of the same year, American and Delta also ordered aircraft, bringing the total number requested to eighty 767-200s, with an additional seventy-nine on option.

With orders and options standing at 159, the 767 program met the 100-plane requirement needed for

This freshly painted All Nippon Airways 767 is ready to head off and join its siblings flying routes out of Tokyo. Like American Airlines, All Nippon is also a heavy user of 767s, with eight -200s and fifty-one -300s. *Boeing*

The flight deck of the 767 was state of the art in the 1980s and a glimpse of things to come. Today's modern cockpits have been taken a step further with nearly all gauges being replaced with large, flat-panel LCD screens. *Boeing*

launch. Holding large orders from three of America's biggest airlines, the Boeing board overlooked its need for a foreign airline order and committed Boeing to full production. At the same time, the 767-100 option was dropped due to lack of interest, and the 767MR/LR was shelved, later to be redesigned as an all-new airliner, the 777.

In July 1979, Boeing and its subcontractors started building parts for the first 767. Companies from all over the world labored for nearly two years preparing their factories and manufacturing the first components for the 767. Once complete and thoroughly checked, thousands of parts and subassemblies were sent to Boeing at its facility in Everett, Washington. Final

Gulf Air, a multinational airline of Bahrain, Oman, Qatar, and the United Arab Emirates, operates a fleet of nine 767-300ERs. Pictured here is one of its aircraft just prior to delivery in June 1988. *Boeing*

assembly started in April 1981, and Boeing rolled out its first widebody twin on August 4, 1981.

The initial model was the -200 series, seating 18 passengers in first class and 198 in coach for a total of 216. There was also an option for seating up to 290 passengers in an all-coach configuration. Typical first-class seating was arranged six abreast, with the isles dividing the seats in a 2-2-2 arrangement. The coach cabin normally had seven abreast in a 2-3-2 formation. The greatest benefit of having a 2-3-2 setup was that

the airliner could be filled to 80 percent capacity without making anyone sit in a less-than-desirable middle seat, as all but 20 percent of seats were beside an aisle or window. Some airlines opted to forgo this convenience in order to pack in more seats for high-density operations, resulting in a less popular, eight abreast, 2-4-2 layout.

No major problems were encountered on the 767's maiden flight on September 26, 1981. The crew did, however, have trouble with a valve that was part of

The size of the General Electric CF6-80C2, one of the primary powerplants used on the 767, is shown here to good effect. The CF6 series produces 52,500 pounds of thrust on the 767-200 and up to 60,800 pounds on the 767-400ER. *General Electric Aircraft Engines*

the vacuum-flushing lavatory system. It failed in flight and made a lot of noise. The crew also encountered a glitch in one of the hydraulic systems, prompting them to keep the landing gear down and locked for the whole flight as a precaution. Despite the minor problems, the test flight landed safely. These issues were quickly resolved, and on July 30, 1982, the 767 received its FAA-type certificate, the highly coveted U.S. government approval signifying a design is safe and airworthy. Just three weeks later, Boeing delivered the first 767 to United Airlines. The company put its new airliner into revenue service on its Chicago to Denver route on September 8, 1982.

Over the next three years, Boeing delivered 767s to more than 100 customers, including some of the largest airlines in the world. United continued to take

An American Airlines 767 "Luxury Liner" rolls out after touchdown. The lack of paint highlights the use of aluminum versus composites on the airframe. The engine cowlings, radome, and wing-to-body fairing are all composite.

An Air New Zealand 767-200ER sits on the ground at Melbourne, Australia. This airliner, ZK-NBA, was the airline's first 767, delivered in September 1985 to its headquarters in Auckland. *Peter Sweetten, Flying Images Worldwide*

As its landing gear retracts, this 767-300ER climbs out of Miami on a flight to Santiago. LanChile is the largest airline in Chile. Until recently it operated an all-Boeing fleet of 737s and 767s. The airline is putting A320s and A319s into service as well.

A Martinair 767-300ER shows the unique position of its main landing gear just prior to touchdown. Aircraft spotters often look for gear tilted this way when trying to distinguish 767s from other widebody twin jets. Martinair is a Dutch airline based in Amsterdam.

Two rivals, the Airbus A330-200 and A330-300, often compete with the 767 for long-range twin jet orders from airlines. The A330 series typically carries 250 to 350 passengers, while the 767s can accommodate 180 to 250. Because of their capacity differences, the 767s can profitably cover less populated city pairs, while the A330s have the advantage on busier routes.

deliveries, and Boeing began to fill the 50 launch orders from Delta and American. TWA took its first 767 delivery in November 1982 and ultimately signed up for nine more aircraft. The 767 also sold well to airlines outside the United States. In the first few years of the program, Boeing exported aircraft to Air Canada, All Nippon Airways of Japan, Ansett Australia, China Airlines, Transbrasil Airlines, El Al Israeli Airlines, Britannia Airways, Ethiopian Airlines, and Egypt Air. By any measure, the program was going well. What Boeing didn't know was that it was about to get even better.

Before the creation of the 767, the FAA restricted twin-engine passenger aircraft from flying more than 90 minutes over water. This was to ensure that the aircraft could safely make it to a runway on their remaining engine if one were to fail. Due to the demonstrated reliability of new generation turbofans like those found on the 767, in June 1985, the FAA increased the statutory safety margin for twin-engine aircraft operating over water. (The maximum allowable distance from the nearest airport was extended to 120 minutes flying time, provided the airline could prove in-flight

Balair, a Swiss charter airline, uses the sides of some of its 767-300ERs as flying billboards for Internet service provider Blue Window. This airplane is pictured in Zurich, home base for the airline. *Michael Pellaton, Flying Images Worldwide*

KLM's 767-300ER *Brooklyn Bridge* stands by to take another load of passengers from Amsterdam to New York. The Dutch airline named each of its 767s after famous bridges, including *Golden Gate Bridge*, *Tower Bridge*, *King Hussein Bridge*, and *Bosporus Bridge*. Note the ETOPS label on the nose gear door.

El Salvador's TACA International Airlines leases four 767s to help connect the city of San Salvador to the rest of the world. Note the U.S. registration, a feature found on all of TACA's aircraft. *Flying Images Worldwide Collection*

Boeing's newest addition to its 767 line is the 767-400ER. Introduced in 2000, it features a fuselage stretch, a 777-style interior, a new flight deck, and raked wing tips. The paint scheme features illustrations from Greek mythology and drawings by Leonardo da Vinci. *Boeing*

Range Capability from Los Angeles

Full Passenger Payload

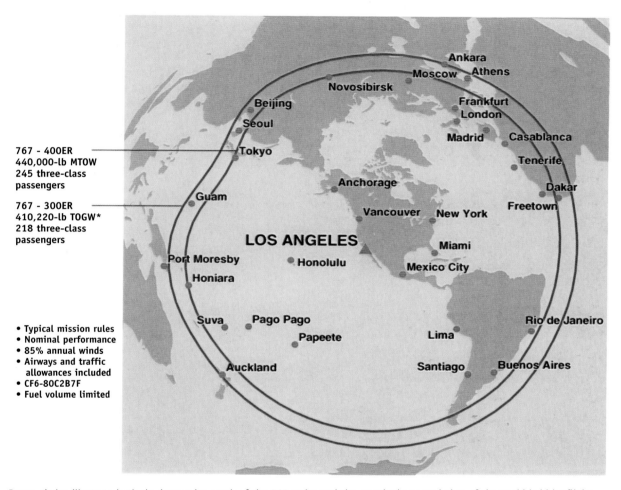

767 - 400ER
440,000-lb MTOW
245 three-class
passengers

767 - 300ER
410,220-lb TOGW*
218 three-class
passengers

- Typical mission rules
- Nominal performance
- 85% annual winds
- Airways and traffic
  allowances included
- CF6-80C2B7F
- Fuel volume limited

LOS ANGELES

Ankara
Moscow   Athens
Novosibirsk
Frankfurt
Beijing   London
Seoul   Madrid   Casablanca
Tokyo   Tenerife
Anchorage   Dakar
Guam   Freetown
Vancouver   New York
Miami
Port Moresby   Honolulu   Mexico City
Honiara
Suva   Pago Pago   Rio de Janeiro
Papeete   Lima
Auckland   Santiago   Buenos Aires

Range circles illustrate both the impressive reach of the 767 series and the seemingly warped view of the world held by flight planners. Starting from Los Angeles, aircraft can reach most of South America, western Europe, and northwestern Africa. Note the best way to reach Moscow from Los Angeles is to fly over the North Pole.

One of the main selling features of the 767-400 is its 777-style interior. Newly sculpted sidewalls, ceilings, and stow bins contribute to a more open feeling. The -400 kept the seven-abreast seating in coach because it places 87 percent of the seats next to a window or aisle. Pictured here are some happy models populating first class for a publicity photo. *Boeing*

engine shutdowns were extremely rare. This 30-minute increase for aircraft practicing extended-range twin-engine operations, or ETOPS, enabled aircraft like the 767 to fly efficient trans-Atlantic routes legally. Just three years later, the allowable limit was extended further to 180 minutes.

Suddenly airlines had the option to operate smaller twin-engine airplanes on less-traveled routes and the ability to make money with moderate payloads. Prior to the rule, only larger three- or four-engine aircraft could fly transatlantic routes, forcing airlines to service only selected major hubs that could generate enough passengers to make the route profitable with such large fuel-hungry aircraft. The miserly 767 could carry passengers from New York to London using only 60 gallons of fuel per passenger. By comparison, an average economy car would have needed 120 gallons to make the trip on a hypothetical road.

Airlines quickly began operating 767s on ETOPS routes everywhere across the Atlantic. In the years leading up to the ETOPS rule change, Boeing was averaging about 15 to 20 sales of the 767 per year. Once the FAA lengthened the ETOPS time, 767 sales quickly jumped to more than 40 per year as airlines scrambled to add ETOPS-equipped 767s to their fleets.

The ongoing success of the 767 program was substantial. From 1976 to 1997, Boeing's original 767 spawned six different variants, the addition of which helped breathe new life into the program. Boeing found the most popular 767 was not the original version. When regulations changed and began allowing the aircraft to work long, over-water routes, demand for extended-range and expanded-capacity 767s increased. The first derivative was the 767-200ER, basically a -200 with 3,750 gallons more fuel capacity and a higher gross weight. The added fuel gave the -200ER 6,770 nautical miles of range, versus the range of 3,850 nautical miles on the standard -200. After airlines were offered an extended-range model, Boeing worked to provide increased capacity. It came up with the 767-300, basically a -200 stretched by 21 feet to allow seating for 45 additional passengers. With a range of 4,260 nautical miles, it could go farther than the -200 but not as far as the -200ER. Naturally, airlines said they wanted more capacity and range, so Boeing developed a long-range version of the 767-300 called the 767-300ER. It could go up to 6,060 nautical miles and quickly became the company's most popular model. In 2002, the -300ER delivery count stood at 459, meaning it had generated more sales than the rest of the 767 versions combined.

767 Orders and Deliveries Summary by Model			
Model Series	No. of Customers	Total Orders	Total Deliveries
767-200	17	128	128
767-200ER	29	117	112
767-300	7	104	104
767-300ER	42	505	471
767-300F	5	40	40
767-400ER	2	37	37
Totals	66*	931	892

ER = Extended Range   F = Freighter   * Individual customers
Cumulative through December 2002   Source: Boeing

Boeing aims to continue the success of its stretched, long-range 767s with the recently offered 767-400ER. Taking the common practice of fuselage stretch to new levels, the -400ER is 21 feet longer than the -300ER and an astonishing 51 feet longer than the original -200. Delta placed the launch order for the aircraft, a request of 21 firm orders, 24 options, and 25 "rolling" options with moving exercise dates.

With the 767 order book likely to exceed 1,000 aircraft, Boeing has gone far beyond the 128-aircraft market predicted for the basic -200 series. By spawning 767 derivatives with increased range, capacity, and performance, the company leveraged its original design into additional markets, and, as some would argue, it even created new areas of demand.

The 767 is a success in itself, but the program also spawned the idea for a future Boeing widebody. Boeing shelved the concept known as the 767MR/LR, a 200-seat trijet with intercontinental range, early in the program. The idea was never completely discarded but was set aside for later use. It sat on the shelf for more than a decade before Boeing picked it up again when it was looking for a new product around the same size. The company dusted it off and headed back to the drawing board, albeit with a head start. The 777 was about to be born.

chapter 3

777
Triple Seven Revolution

"The airlines of the world told us they wanted an airplane that was bigger than the 767 and smaller than the 747," said Alan Mulally, Boeing's director of engineering and future 777 project manager. In 1986, Boeing started to realize the potential of such an airliner. The airlines were troubled by the amount of passenger traffic on some of the city pairs they flew. They could not get enough people to fill up a 747 yet had too many for a 767. In addition, hundreds of older McDonnell Douglas DC-10s and Lockheed L-1011s needed to be replaced by aircraft of similar size. This helped expand the market potential enough for Boeing to think seriously about a new airliner.

The least expensive way for Boeing to accommodate the 300-seat category was to modify the 767 into a larger derivative, complementing the existing line of 767-200s and 767-300s. Armed with this idea, Boeing repeatedly attempted to sell the airlines a new version of the 767 based on its previously envisioned 767MR/LR. Boeing tried giving it new wings, installing new engines, stretching it to various sizes, and combining all of these features but had no luck getting the airlines to bite on the new aircraft. They even pitched a double-decked model. Boeing just could not alter the 767 enough to meet the airlines' needs.

Celebrating the turn of the century, Continental Airlines dressed up one of its 777-200s in special paint. The livery recognizes New York City as "The Millennium Capital of the World."

Tipping the scales at more than 600,000 pounds, the 777 is the largest twin ever built. The -200 series, pictured here, is 209 feet long and has a wingspan just under 200 feet. Typical seating is for 305 passengers in three classes or up to 440 in a high-density configuration.

By 1988, Boeing recognized that it had stalled and was falling behind. McDonnell Douglas was already working on the MD-11, and Airbus was busy with the A330 and A340. The two companies were attempting to fill the 300-seat market niche, forcing Boeing to regroup, and quickly.

Rather than just sending people to talk to the airlines one at a time, Boeing put together a special type of focus group. Representatives from United, American, Delta, British Airways, Japan Air Lines, All Nippon Airways, Qantas, and Cathay Pacific Airways accepted invitations to become intimately involved in developing Boeing's next airliner. Boeing called the group the "Gang of Eight." Boeing and the Gang of Eight spent a year discussing design inputs for the new plane. Boeing took the design inputs and carefully interpreted them for accuracy, at the same time welcoming the Gang of Eight to scrutinize each interpretation. Rarely had the cliche "getting on the same page" been so applicable.

Slowly the details began to emerge. The consensus among the airlines was for their new aircraft to be big widebody twins. Cathay Pacific wanted an airliner with a fuselage as wide as that of a 747, not the size found on the narrower 767 "semi-widebody." The company wanted to be able to have higher passenger loads on its busy Asian routes. American Airlines wanted an airliner with a wingspan comparable to a DC-10 so it could use its existing airport gates, especially at its crowded Dallas hub. Boeing was planning to have a 199-foot wingspan on the 777, rather than a 170-foot span like that on the DC-10, so it offered wing tips that folded up before the airliner taxied into the gate. Boeing received a near-continuous stream of advice from the airlines on critical design issues regarding their operations, maintenance, and use by passengers.

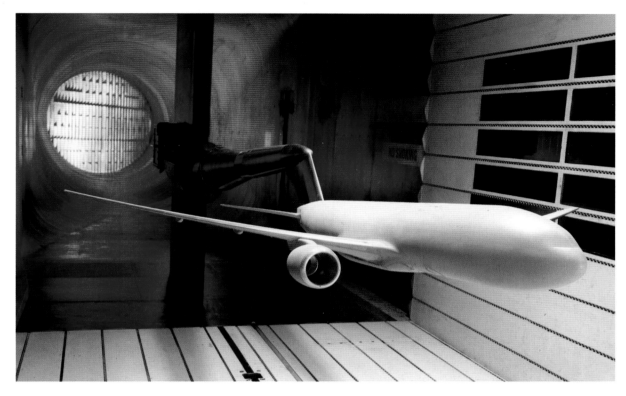

Most of the 777's aerodynamic design was done on computers using computational fluid dynamics. But the computer models had to be validated with wind tunnel tests. Here a 777 model cruises through an artificial sky while engineers study airflow and loads. *Boeing*

In order to facilitate the flow of design information, Boeing created Design Build Teams, or DBTs. Each DBT consisted of a basic cross-functional team from Boeing and a combination of individual supplier, subcontractor, and airline representatives. Teams like these worked on every detail of the 777, whether it was a complex system like the cockpit or just a simple navigation light. There were up to 240 DBTs working on the 777 at one time. For the more complex systems, some DBTs had up to 40 members. DBTs included all the necessary stakeholders from each system so they could easily design components properly from the start. Under the old method, small groups of design specialists created their part, then passed it "over the wall" to the next group, which in turn added its system and passed it along. This process continued, the project passing through several groups until a complete system was ready. The trouble with this method was that any mistakes or requests for changes by the airline customer meant the design would have to start over at thebeginning of the chain. DBTs eliminated thousands of hours of rework and helped Boeing incorporate everyone's needs from the start.

Companies located all around the world produced the 777's three million parts. For example, fuselage panels were assembled in Japan, while the

Forward fuselage panels are positioned adjacent to the nose section prior to final fitting. The airliner's internal structure, which provides remarkable strength despite its light weight, supports the aluminum skin and can be seen on the inside of the far panel. *Boeing*

rudders were built in Australia. Customers were spread across the globe too. Teams often met in Seattle, but Boeing quickly realized that it needed to facilitate worldwide communications. The answer was to design an entire airliner on computers, making Boeing the first manufacturer to do so. Boeing called it the "paperless airplane." At the height of the design process, Boeing had more than 2,200 workstations networked into eight IBM 3090-600J mainframe computers. The setup included a digital design system called Computer-Aided Three-Dimensional Interactive Applications, or CATIA. Using CATIA, Boeing could input three-dimensional designs into the system and check for fit or interference with surrounding parts. This minimized the element of surprise. No longer would Boeing find out on final assembly that a wire bundle and a hydraulic line were both to go through a hole that was actually only big enough for one or the other. With conflicts resolved in advance, contractors could confidently transfer the approved computer models directly to automated manufacturing machines. These machines would build parts with tolerances measured in thousandths of an inch. In final assembly, parts snapped together with ease.

As the 777 design progressed, United and many other airlines told Boeing they wanted an advanced jetliner with "fly-by-wire" flight controls and a computerized "glass" cockpit. United also wanted its new airliner to be able to fly its Denver to Honolulu route nonstop on a hot day. This requirement was significant in that the 777 would have to be certified for ETOPS from day one, something that had never been done before. Most twin-engine aircraft had to prove their reliability through years of reliable service before being allowed to carry passengers over the world's oceans. Boeing was now being asked to prove a plane's reliability right from the start.

Boeing engineers began to realize the challenge engine makers faced in building a suitable powerplant

The 777's distinctive triple-bogie main gear was over-engineered to keep pavement loading to a minimum. The extra strength allowed Boeing to later stretch the 777-200 into the 777-300 series without needing to add additional gear to support the weight. *Boeing*

for the 777. With a maximum takeoff weight between 500,000 and 600,000 pounds, the 777 would be the biggest twin ever built. The FAA required that all twin-engine airliners have enough power to climb out on a single engine, a safety net should the other engine fail late in a takeoff run. To satisfy this benchmark, each 777 powerplant needed tremendous thrust. In fact, the 777 needed the most powerful airliner engines ever built. In addition, airline demands forced engine makers to meet difficult goals for life-cycle costs, fuel consumption, and

Engineers winch the Pratt & Whitney 4084 onto its pylon to power the first 777. The PW4084 was chosen by launch customer United Airlines and was the first to fly. The 777 was ultimately certified to fly with General Electric and Rolls-Royce engines as well. *Boeing*

price. ETOPS certification complicated things even more by requiring the all-new engine to equal the reliability of the best proven designs.

It was a tall order, but the three biggest engine manufacturers in the world stepped up to the challenge. Pratt & Whitney modified its proven PW4000 series to produce substantially higher thrust, primarily through the use of a bigger fan. The new PW4084 could generate 77,200 pounds of thrust. General Electric took a riskier route by developing the GE90,

a clean-sheet design that cranked out a whopping 92,000 pounds of thrust. The third entrant was Rolls-Royce. It introduced the Trent 800 series. The new model was based on the RB211-524G, and the Trent 890 put out 90,000 pounds of thrust. All three engines promised much greater power than the 50,000-pound thrust engines found on the mighty 747.

The new engines accomplished greater power by having higher bypass ratios than engines found on other airliners. An engine's bypass ratio is the amount of air-

The CATIA computer design system allowed Boeing to check all the structural parts, wiring, hydraulic lines, and other systems before a mockup was built. The software helped identify interference problems and saved countless hours of rework. Here is a CATIA view looking down the fuselage. *Boeing*

This 777-200 cutaway shows a typical interior layout, the structure in the wings and empennage, and the routing of the environmental-control ducts. The main framework of the engine pylon and the engine itself are visible through the pylon fairing and engine nacelle. *Boeing*

flow passing through the fan compared to the amount going through the core. Previous engines typically had an airflow ratio of 5-to-1. The 777 engines offered a ratio of 9-to-1. The new engines had so much power they could propel a lightly loaded 777 from 0 to 60 miles per hour in about six seconds.

PROGRAM LAUNCH

With major systems in place, the 777 design progressed rapidly. But Boeing had yet to commit to its final size and performance numbers. The company knew airlines wanted a widebody twin that was somewhere between the 747 and 767 in size. It also knew that the airliner would need to replace aging DC-10s and L-1011s. And it knew the new model had to outperform the MD-11, A330, and A340, designs already in development. What Boeing didn't know was how to create an airliner that could meet the variety of needs being requested. The airlines' various demands were wide-ranging and sometimes even conflicting. Boeing decided that the ultimate solution was to design several variants of a single design, and it ultimately came up with a family of aircraft, as shown below.

Type	Range	Passemgers (1, 2, 3 classes)
The Proposed 777 Family		
A	Medium	440, 375, 305
B	Long	440, 375, 305
Stretch A	Medium	550, 451, 368
Stretch B	Very Long	440, 375, 305

These early model designations were later converted into more commonly seen numbered "dash" variants. The A and B market aircraft became the 777-200 and 777-200ER, respectively, while the Stretch A and Stretch B models were launched years later as the 777-300 and 777-300ER.

As design aspects of the new 777 series solidified, United's need to replace its aging DC-10s became increasingly urgent. The older its DC-10s got, the more maintenance they required. In the airline business, each aircraft grounded for repairs is an enormous blow to company revenues. The DC-10s were spending an increasing amount of time in the hangar. United was also concerned its competitors might start operating efficient new aircraft from other manufacturers and feared their lowered operating costs would allow them to cut ticket prices and lure away its passengers. The airline quickly solicited bids from Boeing, McDonnell Douglas, and Airbus for the 777, MD-11, and A330, respectively, to begin negotiations for its fleet renewal. Boeing incorporated everything it had learned up

to that point into its 777 proposal and gave United its best sales pitch. Boeing proposed the biggest, most fuel-efficient twin-engine airliner ever conceived, and the company was prepared to transform itself radically in order to build it.

Boeing's approach worked. United announced its intentions to order the 777 in October of 1990, selecting it over the MD-11 and A330. The airline signed a letter of intent for thirty-four 777-200s, with options on thirty-four more. To seal the deal, Boeing executives signed a highly unusual, handwritten document that had been conceived in the middle of the night by Jim Guyette, United's vice president of operations. Guyette

The No. 1 Boeing 777 soars through a clear sky on one of its many test flights. Boeing put the 777 through one of the most comprehensive test programs in aviation history. In the first ten months of the program, the 777 endured flutter tests to assess how its structure responded to high speeds; low-altitude ground-effect tests to evaluate the airplane's handling; minimum takeoff speed tests; brake tests; stability and control tests; and configuration deviation tests. And that was only the beginning. *Boeing*

In October 1990, United launched the future of the 777 with its initial request for 34 aircraft and options for 34 more, ordering them to replace its oldest DC-10s. All of United's 777s are Pratt-powered (PW4084 or PW4090) and are -200 series models. N774UA uses its 4084s to power through the mountains on a photo flight. *Boeing*

came up with the document to convince his own chairman and chief financial officer to vote for the 777 rather than the A330, the option toward which United had been leaning. Titled "B.777 Objectives," it said:

In order to launch on-time a truly great airplane, we have a responsibility to work together to design, produce, and introduce an airplane that exceeds the expectations of flight crews, cabin crews, and maintenance and support teams, and ultimately our passengers and suppliers.

From day one:
- *Best dispatch reliability in the industry*
- *Greatest customer appeal in the industry*
- *User friendly and everything works*

Boeing executives pledged to fulfill these promises to United. Guyette took the signed document to United's chairman and said, "This is the new Boeing. The new Boeing is going to treat us at a new level of respect as a customer, and for the next five years they are going to work with us to deliver something Boeing's never delivered before on any other airplane." Of course, hundreds of pages of complex contracts with all the necessary legalese were filled out later. But in a very sincere way, the single-sheet agreement represented the new approach to working together that launched the 777.

United's order for up to sixty-eight 777s would have been worth more than $8 billion to Boeing at market prices. But United did not pay this much, as launch orders are typically steeply discounted. Even with the discounts, Boeing still had a several-billion-

The prototype 777 gets some finishing touches in the paint shop. Painting a simple stripe on a 777 requires a minimum of 850 feet of tape and covering to protect the rest of the aricraft from overspray. Note the prototype's "experimental" placard above the door. *Boeing*

The GE90-94B engine, with 93,700 pounds of thrust, powers the 777-200ER and the 777-300. Without its tailpipe, this engine has a dry weight of 16,644 pounds. The GE90-115B, a growth version of this engine, puts out a staggering 115,000 pounds of thrust, making it the most powerful turbofan ever built. *General Electric Aircraft Engines*

dollar order in its books. The 777 program had logged its first success and was now set to revolutionize the widebody airliner market. But first, Boeing had to prove the 777 could fly.

June 12, 1994, was the day, and Everett's Paine Field was the place. Chief test pilot John Cashman was in command, assisted by director of flight test Ken Higgins. Their Pratt & Whitney–powered 777

was loaded with 34,000 pounds of test equipment wired to collect 50,000 measurements, including speed, altitude, hydraulic pressures, electrical signals, and temperatures throughout the aircraft. The measurements were delivered real-time via satellite telemetry-links to 50 engineers manning consoles in a test-flight command center. Every detail was watched continuously during the maiden flight. The

Continental Airlines and British Airways 777s board passengers at Newark International Airport in New Jersey. Newark is one of the major airports serving New York City. Note the pre-September 11 Manhattan skyline in the background. Until that day, no one had used an airliner as a weapon.

The massive size of the GE90 quickly becomes apparent if you compare it to the fueling truck filling this British Airways 777. The airline surprised the industry when it selected the GE90 over the Rolls-Royce Trent 800 series to power its 777s. British Airways and Rolls are both headquartered in England, and the airline was expected to favor its hometown team.

Boeing was extremely pleased to land a 777 order from Singapore Airlines, an airline known for its large modern fleet and exemplary service. Singapore chose Rolls-Royce to power its fleet of 777s, including this -300 taxiing at Melbourne, Australia. *Peter Sweetten, Flying Images Worldwide*

777 also had a 48-barrel water ballast system inside the cabin to represent passenger and baggage weight and to simulate changes in the center of gravity. The water barrels resembled beer kegs and were even decorated with labels from local microbreweries.

The weather was overcast, and a 15-knot tailwind blew down the runway when the 777 began its takeoff roll. The crew throttled the engines up to 77,000 pounds of thrust, rather than the 74,000 pounds planned, in order to build up enough speed to overcome the tailwind. The 777's ample power easily met the challenge, and the plane lifted off into the cloudy sky. Bad weather kept the 777's altitude between 15,000 and 18,000 feet for most of the flight, but the restriction did not delay any tests. One of the most

important parts of the first flight was to test the fly-by-wire system, and the 777 performed as expected.

One of the more unusual in-flight tests involved shutting down the left engine at 15,000 feet and 240 knots, allowing it to cool, then restarting it with a windmill relight. It worked as planned. All twin-engine airliners had been designed for in-flight shutdowns and restarts, although most never executed such a test on their first flight. Such was the confidence in the 777. The initial test flight lasted 3 hours, 45 minutes. The 777 landed safely and taxied back to smiling Boeing employees.

The successful test flight was only the beginning of the most comprehensive test program ever endured by a new airliner design. Nine 777s were allocated to

the flight development program. Three were dedicated to standard certification flying. The remaining six were assigned to the three engine programs, with two aircraft allocated to each one. Each engine manufacturer used one aircraft for normal engine certification and one for the required 1,000-cycle validation program. The cycle validation program ran each engine-airframe combination to verify the ETOPS design features. This ensured all primary systems worked and that backup systems would kick in properly in the event of a failure. The test program took nearly two years, during which the nine 777s surpassed 7,000 hours while completing more than 4,900 flights. The tests caught a few minor problems, all of which were quickly fixed. The 777 emerged victorious and was granted simultaneous certification from the FAA and the European Joint Aviation Authorities, or JAA, on April 19, 1995. ETOPS certification quickly followed. The 777 entered airline service on June 7, 1995, when a United 777-200 left London Heathrow Airport and flew to Washington, D.C. The aircraft landed at Washington Dulles International Airport 30 minutes ahead of schedule. Boeing's new product was now officially in the game.

ONGOING SUCCESS

From the start, Boeing planned for the 777 program to evolve into a family of aircraft. The first offspring of the original 777-200 was the extended range, or ER, version. The -200ER was given the go-ahead in October 1990, just one year after the initial 777

With a cross section just over 20 feet wide, the 777 is sized neatly between the 21-foot-wide 747 and the 16.5-foot-wide 767. The 777 was Boeing's first airliner to employ a perfectly circular cross section, as all of its predecessors were oval-shaped.

Lauda Air is an Austrian carrier based in Vienna that operates a fleet of four 777-200s powered by GE90-92Bs. Note the airliner's array of communication and navigation antennas mounted along the top of the fuselage. *Peter Sweetten, Flying Images Worldwide*

An American Airlines 777-200 arrives at its gate at London's Heathrow Airport after flying in from Chicago. With its quiet, very high bypass engines, the 777 meets the noise standards at Heathrow, among the most stringent in the world.

Maylasia Airlines flies dozens of Boeing widebodies out of its hub in Kuala Lumpur. Its fleet includes the 777-200 (pictured), 777-300, 747-200F, 747-300, and 747-400. The company also flies A330-300s and an MD-11F. All of its 777s are Rolls-Royce powered. *AJ Smith, Flying Images Worldwide*

launch. The airlines could now order a 777 that would go 7,730 nautical miles, an increase from the 5,210 nautical mile range. They could now fly nonstop from Chicago to Seoul or Los Angeles to Tokyo. The -200ER first flew in October 1996, and it entered service with British Airways in February 1997.

Having answered the airlines' call for more range, Boeing built the next 777 derivative to add capacity. Boeing green-lighted the project in June 1995. To make the -300 series, Boeing took a -200 and stretched it by adding a ten-frame plug forward of the wing and a nine-frame plug at the rear of the aircraft, extending the fuselage by a total of 33 feet, 9 inches. The longer cabin provided space for up to 67 additional passengers in a typical three-class seating configuration. The -300 entered service in May 1998 after delivery to launch customer Cathay Pacific Airways.

Within three years of the 777's first scheduled flight, Boeing had two additional models in service. The company was doing its best to diversify its 777 offerings in order to maximize sales. It was the quick-est way to recoup the enormous expense of development. The following table outlines the progress made by each of the 777 models:

777 Orders and Deliveries Summary by Model

Model Series	No. of Customers	Total Orders	Total Deliveries
777-200	10	86	81
777-200ER	31	407	299
777-200LR	2	5	0
777-300	9	65	44
777-300ER	8	56	0
Totals	36*	619	424

ER=Extended Range   LR = Longer Range   * Individual customers

Cumulative through December 2002   *Source: Boeing*

It is interesting to note the -200ER, not the original -200, garnered the most orders. As with the 767, the launch model was not the most popular. Yet again, Boeing's strategy of diversifying the product line reaped billions of dollars for the company.

A340-200

A340-300

A340-500

A340-600

The A340 line is a direct competitor of Boeing's 777. Four models, ranging from the 239-seat A340-200 to the 380-seat A340-600, offer airlines a variety of sizes from which to choose. Despite ETOPS rule changes based on the proven safety of twins, Airbus markets its four-engine A340s as the safest alternative for long, over-water routes. Boeing says modern turbofans are so reliable only two are needed.

A clean plane is a happy plane. A maintenance worker uses the copilot's side window to access the front windshield of this Delta Air Lines 777-200 for a little pre-flight polish. Airliner windshields are heated, defrosted, and have wickedly fast wipers; but they don't typically have automatic washers.

A British Airways 777-200 takes on freight pallets in its rear cargo hold. The 777's wide cross section also allows it to carry LD3 containers in tandem rows. If an airline wanted to put still more cargo aboard, it could order a 777 with a huge cargo door for unimpeded access to the main deck.

If range was a good thing, then more range would spur even more orders. At least that's what Boeing was hoping when it launched two longer-range 777 models in February 2000. The -200LR was an extended range -200ER, while the -300ER was a longer range -300. Boeing made significant modifications to the base models to get the needed performance. Extended wings with raked wingtips, additional fuel tanks, strengthened gear and brakes, and bigger engines were just a few of the changes. The results were impressive. The -300ER could fly more than 7,100 nautical miles nonstop, allowing direct routes such as that from Los Angeles to Cairo. The -200LR, with a range greater than 8,800 nautical miles, could go even farther and became the longest-range commercial airliner available. It had the ability to fly nonstop between almost any two cities on Earth.

The 777 was the pinnacle of jetliner development in the twentieth century. Its advanced design, modern materials, innovative engines, and extraordinary performance earned it the most prestigious award given for American aerospace achievement. In 1995, the 777 team was awarded the Robert F. Collier Trophy for its remarkable creation.

Boeing had come out on top and was reaping rewards. Over at Douglas, Boeing's major American rival, things couldn't have been worse. The imbalance between the two companies favored Boeing so much that an opportunity arose for Boeing to buy its competitor. And that's precisely what it did.

This scene would have been much less tense had Boeing known what a huge success the 777 would ultimately become. With chase cars poised off each wing, the No. 1 777 is poised for its first takeoff. Its eventual departure opened a powerful new chapter in aviation history.

chapter 4

DC-10 and MD-11
Trijet Inheritance

Boeing's acquisition of McDonnell Douglas in August 1997 meant it now owned an entire line of products it once fiercely competed against. The biggest additions were Douglas's widebody aircraft programs for the DC-10 and MD-11. While production of the DC-10 had ended in 1989, the MD-11 line was still trickling along and turning out new aircraft. As its new owner, Boeing had to decide what to do with the line. On one hand, Boeing could close down the assembly line and remove the MD-11 from the market to boost sales of its own widebodies. On the other hand, Boeing could get more out of its investment by continuing to build MD-11s. The company first needed to figure out if the newly acquired MD-11s would actually sell. To decide, Boeing looked closely at the history of the program.

The genesis of the DC-10 dated back to 1966. Like Boeing, Douglas had competed for the CX-HLS contract to build the next giant airlifter for the U.S. military and lost to Lockheed. But in defeat, Douglas studied other uses for the new airlifter's giant high-bypass turbofans, just as Boeing had done. The engines promised power unlike anything ever seen

As they fade from the glory days of airline service, many DC-10s are finding a new life hauling freight. Many have gone to Federal Express, the world's largest integrated package delivery company. This aging FedEx DC-10-10 will soon undergo a complete cockpit makeover and return to service as an MD-10, with a fully digital two-crew cockpit.

A Sun Country Airlines DC-10-15 approaches its home base at Minneapolis-St. Paul International Airport. Only seven DC-10-15s were ever built. The Series 15 was just like a Series 10, but with higher thrust CF6 engines offering 46,500 pounds instead of 41,000.

before. Boeing had used them to come up with the design for the gigantic 747. Douglas designers envisioned using them in their own widebody aircraft. Although Douglas didn't know it at the time, it had an ally over at American Airlines, where Frank Koch was vice president of engineering. He was responsible for determining what type of airliners his company would need and was assigned to work with manufacturers to get them. He was also watching the development of the new engines with great interest.

Koch had visions of a large new airplane, but his idea was for something a little smaller than the behemoth Boeing was working on. He wanted an airliner with widebody comfort that used the new high-bypass turbofans, but preferred one sized somewhere between the earlier 707 and the 747. Koch specified that

American Airlines needed "aircraft with 220 to 230 seats in a mixed-class configuration and a range of 1,850 nautical miles." Because American operated a large number of flights between New York and Chicago, Koch also wanted the new plane to be light enough to operate out of New York's LaGuardia airport where the runway weight limit was 270,000 pounds. Koch believed a widebody twin was the best solution for meeting this set of parameters. He called the concept the "Jumbo Twin." Others labeled it the "Airbus," a name that would later gain fame on a similarly configured European airliner project.

Douglas was eager to get started, but the late 1950s and early 1960s were marked by company cash-flow problems. The DC-8 series and the DC-9 series were doing well, but both had come at great

Northwest Airlines opted for Pratt & Whitney–powered DC-10s. Douglas originally called the Pratt-powered aircraft DC-10-20s. However, Northwest wanted to appear more modern than the other airlines flying DC-10-30s. Thus, from that point on, the DC-10-20 became the DC-10-40 (pictured).

development expense. Douglas had not had enough time to recoup its investments, and in 1966 it needed $400 million just to meet its financial commitments. During the same period, it also lost some important military contracts to build fighters for the U.S. Air Force. A huge new widebody aircraft program was the company's best hope. Unfortunately, it would cost hundreds of millions of dollars to develop, and the company was in no position to issue more debt. Stuck in a quandary in which the only way to get out of debt was to spend a lot more money, Douglas hired financial analysts to crunch the numbers and offer solutions. The analysts could only come up with one plan. Douglas had to seek a merger.

In early 1967, McDonnell Corporation, a large American military-aircraft manufacturer, completed the acquisition and created McDonnell Douglas Corporation, making Douglas Aircraft Company a division of the newly formed corporation. The new firm was now the fourth-largest American aircraft manufacturer, behind Boeing, North American, and Lockheed. Armed with new resources and the backing of a new chairman, James McDonnell, who was eager to be in the airliner business, Douglas went in pursuit of its new widebody.

Back at American Airlines, Koch knew it was unlikely that an aircraft manufacturer would build the airliner based on his request alone. Other airlines would have to place orders for a manufacturer to commit the hundreds of millions of dollars needed to build it. Since Boeing was already committed to building the 747 and therefore unlikely to take on another new development project, Koch held his

Compared to the digital flight decks found on the 777 and 747-400, the front office of the DC-10 looks quite dated today. Pilots joke that it is filled with "old-fashioned steam gauges." But back in the 1970s, it was state of the art. Note the group of three throttles on the center console.

initial meetings with Douglas and Lockheed. He found both eager to design a new plane. TWA and Eastern, both major airlines at the time, showed similar enthusiasm and quickly joined in. The additional customers Koch needed had arrived.

The only drawback was that Koch's dream plane would now be subject to new input. The other airlines had additional needs that required modification of

Koch's "Jumbo Twin." Many of TWA's routes crossed the Rocky Mountains, and the FAA would require that any twin flying those routes be able to maintain altitude on a single engine in the event of an engine failure. The new high-bypass engines were powerful, but not that powerful. TWA needed a third engine to ensure safety. Similarly, Eastern flew an important route from New York to Puerto Rico that consisted of

A DC-10 flight engineer sits at this station behind the copilot, monitoring the status of the engines and other systems. Note how identical gauges are clustered in groups of three, giving a readout for each of the plane's three engines. In the MD-11, this station was eliminated by incorporating all of its functions into a digital front panel.

1,800 miles over water. Again, FAA safety rules at the time required at least three engines in case of engine failure far from land, leaving two to be used to make it back to shore. In short order, Koch's "Jumbo Twin" had become an even bigger jumbo trijet.

RIVAL TRIJET

Meanwhile, the management at Lockheed was trying to plot its future. The company had won the CX-HLS contract and was gearing up to build its massive C-5

Galaxies at its production plant in Marietta, Georgia. But its main facility in Burbank, California, was running out of things to do. At the time, it was in the middle of building the four-engine turboprop Electra. Prior to that, the facility was busy cranking out piston-engine Constellations. Faced with a commercial airline market that favored jets and saw supersonic airliners as the future, Lockheed needed a new airliner project if it was going to stay in the business. After losing a supersonic airliner development contract to Boeing in

The DC-10's archrival in the marketplace was the Lockheed L-1011. Both were widebody trijets, the major difference being the placement of the No. 2 engine. Here an ATA L-1011 shows off its approach configuration with high-lift devices deployed and landing gear down. The Rolls-Royce engines remain at idle through flare and touchdown, then power up and reverse thrust to bring the 150-ton airliner to a halt.

December 1966, Lockheed president Daniel Haughton put his development team to work on Koch's jet. Lockheed's design was called L-1011.

With Douglas and Lockheed both working on solving the problems of the same group of airlines, it was no surprise when they came up with very similar widebody trijet configurations. The main difference between the two plans was the placement of the third engine. Both designs had an engine under each wing. Douglas opted for mounting the DC-10's number two engine above the fuselage in the base of the vertical stabilizer, enabling the air feeding the engine to pass straight through an inlet at the front and out a nozzle at the back. Lockheed mounted the L-1011's number two engine lower than the DC-10's, placing it at the

aft-end of the fuselage. Like the DC-10, the L-1011's engine inlet was mounted at the base of the vertical stabilizer, but it used an S-duct to route the air down to the engine and out the back of the fuselage. This seemingly minor difference became a powerful distinction as the competing designs progressed.

The design of the L-1011 required its fuselage-mounted engine to be short in length. The trouble was neither General Electric nor Pratt & Whitney had a small enough engine. Lockheed looked to British engine maker Rolls-Royce, which had been wanting to break into the U.S. airliner market. Rolls-Royce had yet to make significant inroads, so it offered to build Lockheed a turbofan called the RB-211 specifically for the L-1011. The battle for the widebody trijet was set to begin.

Challenge Air Cargo operated DC-10-40 freighters out of Miami before being acquired by UPS. The aircraft, owned by a leasing company, were not part of the acquisition. UPS instead purchased Challenge's equipment, routes, and infrastructure. Acquired during the company's last year of operation, a Challenge Air DC-10-40 reverses thrust after landing.

In February 1968, Douglas launched the first strike by landing a 25-aircraft order from American Airlines, with options for 25 more. The $400 million deal buoyed spirits at Douglas. Landing a deal with such a major U.S. airline would help get the DC-10 program off the ground. However, even if American exercised its options and ultimately took delivery of 50 jets, its business alone couldn't guarantee enough revenue for Douglas to offset the development costs. While Douglas pondered the future of the DC-10 program, Lockheed struck back. The newly powered L-1011 helped Lockheed secure orders from four important customers. Delta, Eastern, TWA, and a British firm called Air Holdings signed up for as many as 168 aircraft. Lockheed was looking at sales worth $2.5 billion.

This news cast a dark cloud over Douglas. Despite the deal with American, it still needed more orders, and Lockheed had just snatched up three of the five largest airlines in the United States. If Douglas could not find a way to sell more DC-10s, James McDonnell would likely abandon the widebody airliner market and have the division focus only on small airliners. In short, Douglas would lose its position in the airline industry. If the firm was to remain a major player, it had to find more customers for the DC-10.

United, the largest U.S. airline at the time, also wanted to buy a fleet of trijet widebodies and had yet to decide on a supplier. Due to the fierce competition between Douglas and Lockheed, United was in a position to demand the most favorable terms for its deal.

The DC-10 was drafted into military service when the United States Air Force bought 60 KC-10A extenders to fulfill its need for a multirole tanker transport. The extender gives combat aircraft wings great mobility by allowing them to transport supplies and personnel while refueling en route. This airplane is based with the 305th and 514th Air Mobility Wings of McGuire Air Force Base in New Jersey.

Although Douglas and Lockheed both wanted the order badly, Douglas needed it more. Douglas cut the price of the DC-10 by $500,000. General Electric was eager to get its engines on the DC-10 and reduced the price for its CF-6, offering it for less than the cost of the Rolls RB-211 on the L-1011. General Electric also used its ties with Morgan Guaranty to help United Airlines finance the deal. The total package was enough to convince United. George Keck, United's president,

called Lockheed with the bad news. Explaining his reasons for choosing Douglas, he said, "If we don't buy that airplane, they will probably drop the DC-10 altogether. And I don't think that's good for Douglas, and I don't think it's good for the country. Douglas might not stay in the business, and I want them in it."

On April 25, 1968, United signed up for 30 DC-10s and took options for 30 more. This meant that Douglas held orders for 55 aircraft and options for 55

The "flying boom," seen here extended from the rear of the plane, allows the KC-10 refueling operator to connect to Air Force fighters and bombers and quickly off-load large quantities of fuel. The KC-10 also has a "hose and drogue" system for refueling U.S. Navy and Marine Corps aircraft, and friendly aircraft from other countries.

The General Electric CF6 is the most popular engine found on DC-10s. Excluding the 42 Pratt-powered DC-10-40s, the CF6 is found on every other aircraft in the fleet. This one, a CF6-50C, was removed for routine maintenance. Soon it will be back in service, pushing a DC-10 with more than 50,000 pounds of thrust.

more. The history of airline orders led Douglas to believe that its customers, the two largest airlines in the United States, would place orders for more in the future as well. Fueled with newfound optimism, the McDonnell Douglas board of directors finally approved the launch of the DC-10 program.

Ultimately, the DC-10 program turned out 466 aircraft. The original design, known as the DC-10-10, was modified into several variants to bring in additional sales. The -30 was the most important of the derivations. It was given a larger wing and had an auxiliary fuel tank in the center body to increase range, making it a true transcontinental performer. In order to cope with the weight of the extra fuel, an additional two-wheel main landing-gear unit was added underneath the wing's center section. More powerful engines allowed it to keep performance up despite the weight gain. Airlines ultimately ordered 233 of the airliners.

The -30 itself spawned additional variants. The -30CF, a convertible freighter, featured removable airline seating for easy conversion from airliner to freighter. A large cargo door on the left front side of the fuselage would enable the -30CF to handle bulky freight. A pure freighter version, the -30F, was also offered. Another -30 spin-off was the -20, essentially a -30, but instead of General Electric CF6s, it was equipped with Pratt & Whitney JT9D engines. Japan Air Lines and Northwest Airlines both favored Pratt engines and ordered the -20 series. In light of other airlines ordering from the -30 series, Northwest wanted a higher designation on its aircraft to help its fleet appear more modern. It pressured Douglas to rename the -20 as the -40. The name change helped convince Northwest to buy 22 of the planes. Japan Air Lines bought 20.

Douglas adapted the DC-10 into a military aircraft as well. Using the -30CF variant as a starting point, engineers added in-flight refueling equipment

The DC-10s have reached the twilight of their career. As the aircraft mature into old age, airlines are slowly selling them off and replacing them with more efficient widebody twins. They'll be around hauling freight for decades, but their glory days of airline service are nearly over.

and seven additional fuel bladders to create a strategic tanker transport, allowing it to refuel fighters and bombers in flight and enabling it to haul military supplies and personnel. Fuel was stored in the wing tanks and in bladders placed in the lower holds, while the main deck carried freight and accommodated up to 75 passengers. The U.S. Air Force liked what it saw in Douglas's design and selected Douglas's tanker, dubbed the KC-10A Extender, in December 1977 over a competing offer from Boeing that was based on a modified 747. The Air Force bought 60 KC-10As from Douglas and continues to use them to support America's interests throughout the world.

ENTER THE ELEVEN

Douglas won many additional orders throughout the 1970s and 1980s by adapting the DC-10 to a variety of roles, but eventually the appeal of its aircraft faded. The introduction of the widebody Airbus A300 in 1974 and the Boeing 767 in 1981 began to erode sales, particularly on domestic routes. The aging trijet just could not compete with the modern twins, which offered advanced engines with greater fuel efficiency and more reliability. The 767 even came with an advanced two-crew cockpit that eased workload for pilots and reduced crew costs for airlines. The DC-10, with its pilot, copilot, and engineer stations, needed three in the cockpit.

An American Airlines MD-11 reaches for touchdown. With its cabin stretch, advanced flight deck, restyled interior, and more powerful engines, the MD-11 was a completely modernized DC-10. Production started in 1991 and lasted until 2001, with 200 aircraft produced. American sold off its last MD-11s in the fall of 2001.

If Douglas wanted to compete in the widebody market in the 1990s and beyond, it needed something more than another DC-10 variant. The company needed something bigger and more advanced than anything it had ever built.

After looking at and then rejecting several clean-sheet designs, Douglas considered radically changing the DC-10-30. Rather than completely reinventing the wheel, Douglas focused on replacing the outdated systems. Stretching the fuselage made sense for increased capacity and range. Douglas also wanted the newest generation of high-bypass turbofans and needed a redesigned cockpit to eliminate the flight engineer station. The company quickly tallied up enough improvements to develop a whole new family of aircraft and named it MD-11.

The MD-11 was officially launched in December 1986. The aircraft design reduced weight and drag. It featured an 18-foot stretch over the standard DC-10-30, a modified tail with less sweepback and integral fuel tanks, winglets on the wingtips, a restyled cabin, and new engine options. Douglas also redesigned the tail to incorporate a low-drag tail cone with a squared-off vertical wedge rather than the conventional rounded cone. A two-crew cockpit was standard. Gone were the dozens of analogue gauges and dials as was the entire flight engineer station. This was all replaced by an integrated six-screen electronic flight-information system neatly arranged across the cockpit. Douglas enlisted pilots from 37 airlines to provide input on how best to automate the cockpit systems. An important safety feature was added to ensure the pilot could overrule automated systems at any time.

The MD-11 was well received by airlines and leasing companies, but it took longer than expected to compile enough orders, causing the board to delay the program launch. After a year of signing up customers, orders for 92 aircraft convinced the McDonnell Douglas board of directors to approve production. However, delays continued to haunt the MD-11. After several planned milestone dates came and went, airlines started to lose faith in the project. Initial orders dropped to 30. Problems with cash flow and production planning moved the program back even more. One by one, Douglas resolved the issues, and the MD-11 took its first flight on January 10, 1990.

Entering the test flight process is often the home stretch of fine-tuning for an airliner, but MD-11 test flights were turning up big problems. The MD-11 was not meeting its performance numbers for range. Douglas did everything it could to minimize drag, increase the efficiency of the engines, and reduce its weight. By redesigning dozens of components and systems, Douglas was able to get the MD-11 to meet its advertised performance range of 7,000 nautical

miles. Ultimately, the MD-11 became the most advanced widebody trijet ever built.

Unfortunately, the bumpy road of development and the talk of performance problems took their toll on the MD-11 program. Orders came in, but the numbers were not anywhere near those forecasted. Douglas predicted selling 300 planes when it first embarked on the MD-11 project, but only 200 were ordered. And those orders were placed only after Douglas developed several variants to broaden the market. To entice airlines that wanted to haul both passengers and freight, Douglas developed the MD-11 Combi to hold 216 passengers in typical two-class seating and 16 freight pallets on the main deck. Only five Combis were sold. For those airlines wanting to fly longer distances, Douglas developed the MD-11ER. It added fuel and aerodynamic improvements to offer 200 nautical miles more range. A pure freight version, the MD-11F, became popular with a number of cargo airlines, attracting orders for 59 aircraft. However, it took more than ten years to solicit that number of requests. By the late 1990s, sales of all variants slowed to just a trickle.

After buying out Douglas in 1997, Boeing continued to market the MD-11 for a year. Boeing had a few successes, especially with the MD-11F freighter. Federal Express, a long-time customer of the MD-11F, ordered three aircraft. Lufthansa Cargo made a surprise order for nine freighters, but the MD-11's days were numbered. The future order book was just too bleak. On June 3, 1998, Boeing announced it was phasing out the MD-11 for good. It was hard to lezt the world's ultimate trijet go, but doing so allowed Boeing to focus its efforts on developing new aircraft for the twenty-first century.

chapter 5

THE SONIC FUTURE?

Entering the twenty-first century, Boeing faced stiff competition from Airbus. As a result, Boeing redoubled its efforts to determine how to win more orders. The company knew it could not continue indefinitely building derivatives of existing models. Looking to the future, Boeing realized it would need an all-new design to maintain a competitive edge. This would be an enormous challenge, but Boeing took solace in the fact that Aribus was facing similar problems.

In December 2000, Airbus announced its new strategy, telling the world it would invest $12 billion to build a new airliner larger than the mighty 747. Airbus wanted a complete product line to challenge Boeing. The 747's dominance in the heavy aircraft market had always been a sore spot for the company. The new airplane, called the A380, was a double-decked, 550-seat airliner. Airbus trumpeted the A380 as the only "modern" high-capacity design, labeling the 747 "old technology." The fact that the latest 747s had changed substantially since their introduction wasn't mentioned.

Boeing had to respond. It pondered a series of questions. What commercial airliner attribute would offer the best edge? Was it speed, capacity, range, efficiency, ease of production, or something else? What skills and abilities would set its next design apart from Airbus? Was it innovative engineers, computer technology, or perhaps systems integration that would

Currently, the fastest conventional airliners cruise at Mach 0.85. The Sonic Cruiser is a new airliner concept designed to travel just under the speed of sound, with a cruise speed between Mach 0.95 and Mach 0.98. *Boeing*

Not only is it faster, the Sonic Cruiser is also designed to cruise higher than most air traffic, where it can use its speed without gaining on conventional airliners on the airways. By operating up at the mid-40,000-foot level, it can pass over traffic plodding along in the more crowded 30,000-foot to 40,000-foot flight levels. *Boeing*

make the difference? What would keep Airbus from taking away the company's customers? To best exploit the market, Boeing's Commercial Airplane Group needed a new direction.

Boeing considered building its own giant widebody. It studied all-new designs as well as heavily modified derivatives of the 747. The company had looked at double-decked aircraft many times, but a new double-decker or a giant 747 just did not seem to be the answer. Boeing's vision of the changing airliner market was that it would become increasingly fragmented, with airlines expanding the number of smaller aircraft they used on direct routes. Airbus held the opposite view. It saw airlines flying an increasing number of large aircraft into the world's major airport hubs. In the scenario adopted by Airbus, the creation of a huge new airliner

made sense. Boeing, however, was unconvinced, so it began looking through its toolbox for the answer.

In the mid 1990s, Boeing's new airplane development group formed a "20XX" project. Its purpose was to collect configurations, manufacturing systems, and other "tools" it might use to build a new airplane in the twenty-first century.

Boeing latched on to a design idea known as the "Pacific Fragmenter." It was conceived to fragment the trans-Pacific hub system by bypassing large airline hubs and instead flying point-to-point routes at near-sonic speed. The trouble with the design was its traditional mid-fuselage placement of a highly swept wing, which needed an area-ruled fuselage to reduce drag. The fuselage shape, similar to that of an old Coca-Cola bottle, gave the design a varying-width passenger

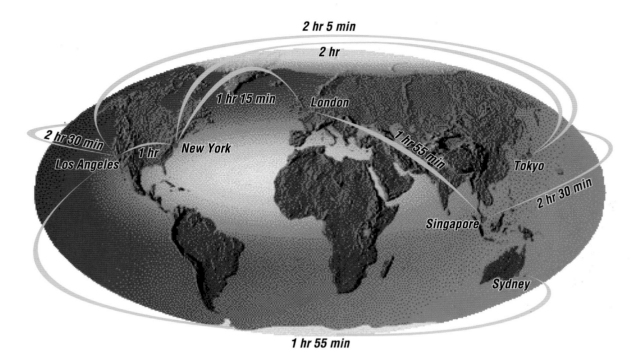

This map shows how much flight time the Sonic Cruiser will save on typical routes. By traveling 15 to 20 percent faster than a conventional jetliner, it can shave hours off international flights. If the Sonic Cruiser and a conventional jet departed simultaneously on a trans-Pacific flight from Los Angeles to Singapore, the Sonic Cruiser would arrive 2 hours and 30 minutes sooner. *Boeing*

compartment, therefore adding structural and manufacturing complexities. The fuselage shape made the plane impossible to stretch or shrink into different sizes without a complete redesign for each. Due to the importance of building derivatives to maximize sales, such a restriction made the design a nonstarter.

To avoid similar problems, Boeing started looking at different configurations for a high-speed aircraft. Boeing's engineers used an innovative new tool known as computational fluid dynamics, or CFD, to help them in the design process. Ever since the days of the Wright brothers, aircraft engineers have treated air as a fluid and have studied how it flows around an aircraft. Using an aircraft model in a wind tunnel, they injected smoke to make the airflows visible. CFD computerized the whole process so that designs could be tested, adjusted, and retested without the expense of wind tunnels and models.

Using CFD, Boeing came up with a new design in late 1999. This design put the wing at the back of the fuselage, which allowed the fuselage to be narrowed as was necessary near the tail of the aircraft. The new configuration solved the manufacturing and internal layout problems of an area-ruled fuselage. The fuselage had a standard, constant cross section just like that on any other airliner, but it could retain the necessary shape to enable high-speed flight without degrading its speed, range, and fuel efficiency. Boeing's new design

Most of the aerodynamic studies for the Sonic Cruiser are done on computers using computational fluid dynamics. However, wind tunnels are used to validate the computer models and run additional tests. The computer models have been found to be accurate within 1 percent. Designing and testing designs on computers enables Boeing engineers to optimize prototypes much faster. *Boeing*

appeared to achieve what no other airliner could—efficient operation at transonic speeds.

When an airplane goes supersonic, it creates a sonic boom. This shock wave of noise follows the aircraft in a cone-shaped pattern wherever it goes. If a supersonic airliner passed over your house, the shock wave would hit moments later, causing a double thunder clap that would rattle your windows and shake the dishes in the cupboards. Obviously such a commotion would be unacceptable if it happened every time an airliner passed overhead. That's why the Concorde has only been allowed to fly supersonic when it is over the ocean. This effectively limits it to over-water routes. Boeing did not want such limits on its new airplane's operation and market potential, so it optimized it to cruise efficiently at Mach 0.98, just below the speed of sound. Due to its near-sonic cruising speed, the plane was quickly dubbed the "Sonic Cruiser."

Boeing saw the potential for the Sonic Cruiser to revolutionize air travel. In early 2001, Boeing began showing its new design to the airlines. It grabbed their immediate attention:

> We obviously see a use for that airplane . . . .
> It can radically change our business productivity.
> *—Donald J. Carty, CEO, American Airlines*

> If it meets the economics, we're going to buy the airplane.
> *—Gordon Bethune, CEO, Continental Airlines*

> This aircraft would represent a very significant additional option.
> *—Leo F. Mullin, CEO, Delta Air Lines*

With airline interest growing, Boeing had to move quickly. The company had the larger 747 in the

Boeing's High Speed Civil Transport concept is an example of a supersonic airliner with an area-ruled fuselage. For aerodynamic efficiency, the fuselage must narrow where it intersects with the wing. A wing placed in the middle of the fuselage results in an irregular-shaped cabin that is difficult to manufacture and expensive to resize into new variants. *Boeing*

works, and it was also planning a longer-range version of the 767-400ER. Rather than wait years for those programs to come to fruition and eventually free up company resources, Boeing quietly elected to cancel them both and focus more energy on the Sonic Cruiser. The company planned to refine its idea and make a formal announcement of the new plane in the fall of 2001. Those plans were dashed when information about the Sonic Cruiser was leaked to the aviation press, supposedly from an airline source. Rather than

leave people guessing, Boeing stepped up and made its announcement early, on March 29, 2001, to be exact.

Alan Mulally, president and CEO of Boeing's Commercial Airplane Group, made the official statement and said, "We have an airplane that will open a new chapter in commercial aviation." Mulally conveyed Boeing's intention to offer airlines a radical new airliner unlike anything ever seen. The Sonic Cruiser would fly economically at near-sonic speeds, substantially faster than an ordinary commercial airlin-

The Sonic Cruiser's wing is mounted at the rear, so its fuselage can taper naturally at its end. The passenger cabin is a constant width, making it easy to build and modify into various lengths. The powerplants may be slight derivatives of 777 engines, possibly with a lower bypass ratio for a more compact fit on the airframe and more exhaust velocity to match the higher cruise speed. *Boeing*

Boeing has built a 20-foot-long composite fuselage section to test candidate materials and manufacturing techniques for the Sonic Cruiser. Other materials and techniques also are being considered. Shown here, the section is readied for Boeing's large anechoic chamber to test the acoustic characteristics. Other tests will determine durability and maintainability. *Boeing*

er. Mulally pointed out that the ability to fly at speeds of Mach 0.95 or faster would allow passengers to arrive quickly where they wanted when they wanted while avoiding congested hubs as well as the hassle and delay of intermediate stops. It was a direct shot at the A380.

A near-sonic airliner is capable of eliminating one hour of flight time on a typical 3,000 nautical-mile route like that from New York to London. A conventional airliner makes this trip in about 6.5 hours. On a longer trip, such as that from Los Angeles to Singapore, a Mach 0.95 or faster airliner can

shorten flight times by 3 hours over the Mach 0.85 747. If the Sonic Cruiser was built with a 10,000 nautical-mile range, it could fly nonstop from London to Syndey and save five hours over the current service needing one stop. The longer the flight, the greater the advantage of the Sonic Cruiser.

Faster flights benefit not only passengers but also the airlines themselves. Getting an airplane on the ground sooner allows it to be unloaded and serviced in time for another revenue-generating flight. On certain city pairs, airlines would be able to use the saved time

The A380, shown here prior to being named, is Airbus's answer to the future of air travel. The massive 550-seat double-decked jumbo will operate on hub-to-hub routes between the world's biggest population centers. While the Sonic Cruiser may operate on these routes as well, it was designed to provide an option to bypass big hubs entirely.

to add one extra flight per day without putting an additional airliner on the route. An airline could use speed as a measure of productivity. With the Sonic Cruiser, Boeing believed that airlines could offer better service to passengers through shorter flight durations and enhance their productivity at the same time.

SONIC REFINEMENT

With the Sonic Cruiser's essential configuration defined, Boeing had to decide carefully how many passengers it could carry. The company already offered a full product line of commercial aircraft ranging from 100 to 400 seats. The new airplane could potentially cannibalize sales from existing products if it were offered at a similar size and range. Boeing knew the

Sonic Cruiser held the most advantage on long-range flights, so it looked at its long-range widebody aircraft for product-line gaps.

Although still popular, 747 sales had slowed. For example, there were 151 orders placed on 747s in mid 1997, but only 77 were on order in mid 2001. Airbus believed the falling orders were due to the 747's old design as well as the competitive pressure exerted by the A380 and its new technology. Boeing had said that it was part of a logical shift toward smaller aircraft, suggesting it would directly serve new city pairings rather than larger ones on busy hub-to-hub routes. If Boeing made its Sonic Cruiser a 400-plus seater, it would directly contradict this position. Although a 747-sized Sonic Cruiser could put enormous pressure

Boeing will enlist about a dozen airlines to help define the fundamental configuration for the Sonic Cruiser, including the plane's range and how many passengers it will carry. From what several airline executives have said in interviews, they are looking for a plane about the size of a 767 that will carry from 200 to 300 passengers with a range of about 9,000 nautical miles. Though it would incorporate the most advanced technologies, the airplane also would fit into the airport infrastructures used to support today's airplanes. *Boeing*

to Airbus and its A380 program, it would not be as lucrative if Boeing's predictions of decreased demand for ultra-large aircraft came true.

The 777 was the next size down from the 747, offering around 350 seats. Boeing had reason to be very optimistic about the 777's prospects. The year 2000 was one of the most successful in terms of the number of aircraft delivered, with 117 rolling off the lines. Such sales ten years after the model's introduction proved

the 777 was a strong player in Boeing's line. Given the projected growth in air travel and Boeing's plans for longer range -200LR and -300ER variants, the future of the 777 looks the brightest of any of Boeing's widebody aircraft programs.

The next step down in size is the 767 at around 200 seats. The ongoing success of the 767 program is substantial, further supporting Boeing's view of smaller aircraft and route fragmentation. The most popular

As Boeing considers the distant future, it might look to a Blended Wing Body design to be its next airliner. Calculations predict a 450-seat BWB design could offer airlines 30 percent lower operating costs than the Airbus A380. *Boeing*

767 is not the original domestic-ranged version. When regulations changed and began allowing twin-engine aircraft to work long-distance, over-water routes, demand for extended-range 767s increased. The 218-seat, longer range 767-300ER has become the most popular model.

With billions of dollars invested in each of its current widebody aircraft programs, Boeing must carefully evaluate any possible effects a new aircraft might have on its current products. Given Boeing's predictions of an increasingly fragmented market with shrinking aircraft sizes, the first offerings of the Sonic Cruiser will likely be in the 250-seat class, placing it just above the 767 models but below the 777 in capacity.

STRATEGY SHIFT

With a target size in mind, Boeing worked toward bringing the Sonic Cruiser to market by 2008. Unfortunately, the market was working against it. A declining 2001 economy put the troubled airline industry deep into the red, and the September 11 terrorist attacks pushed the economic descent into a free fall. The public could not afford to travel as much, and when they could, they were often afraid to fly. "In my 33 years, I have never seen the combination of economic decline and terrorist overhead," said Boeing's Alan Mulally.

Some of America's largest carriers were on the edge of bankruptcy, with no other choice but to apply for federally subsidized loans to stay solvent. United Airlines and U.S. Airways were forced to file Chapter 11 to reorganize. In a struggle to survive, airlines quickly retired their unused aircraft. At one point, up to 2,000 excess airliners were parked in storage in the United States alone. As the airlines deferred or canceled their existing orders, Boeing slowed production of its current models and began to rethink its new airplane strategy. Airlines were simply unable to splurge on a revolutionary new aircraft like the Sonic Cruiser. Boeing market research clearly showed their preferences moving away from speed and toward greater efficiency. In December 2002, Boeing reluctantly shelved the Sonic Cruiser. The company vowed to continue studies and keep up the development effort until the market for it improved, but dropped the project from its high-profile status.

Boeing went back to the drawing board to develop an airplane that better matched airline efficiency needs. Fortunately, a group of Boeing engineers had already been working on one. The study, known as Project Yellowstone, was for a conventional aircraft that offered a 15 to 20 percent increase in operating efficiency over current designs by using advanced technologies developed for the Sonic Cruiser. The aircraft, temporarily dubbed the "super-efficient airplane," seated 200 to 250, had a 7,500-nautical-mile range, and speed that matched the 747 and 777. It offered less noise, lower emissions, and lower fuel burn, making it economical to operate and environmentally friendly. The new aircraft was a more conservative product than the Sonic Cruiser, but it still followed Boeing's vision of increased use of smaller aircraft on fragmented routes.

Boeing announced that the super-efficient airplane would be its next new product after determining there was a market for 2,000 to 3,000 such aircraft over the next twenty years. The company expected the first orders to come from 777 and 767 operators due to their experience working point-to-point routes. Once in service, the super-efficient airplane would replace the 757 and 767 in Boeing's product line. In the broader marketplace, the new aircraft could replace the Airbus A300 and A310, Lockheed L-1011, and DC-10. Boeing planned deliveries to begin in 2008.

Looking to the distant future, another group of Boeing engineers is working on the next generation of airliners called blended-wing-bodies, or BWBs. The BWB design is a highly efficient long-range transport with a wide fuselage that blends into the wing, creating an airliner similar to a flying wing in that the whole airplane generates lift and minimizes drag. The design's unique shape also allows for center-body growth and makes room for additional seats and cargo while retaining the same wings, cockpit, and structure regardless of its size. Boeing is studying a whole series of BWB concepts for airliner use, ranging from 200 to 550 passengers that would offer up to 30 percent savings in fuel over a conventional airliner.

The newest Boeing widebody will soon be waiting at your gate. Whether it's a BWB, a super-efficient airplane, a Sonic Cruiser, or a simple derivative of an existing model, Boeing will research the airline market carefully and produce only what airlines agree to purchase. Critics of this approach, who are frustrated with the conservative nature of most airlines when it comes to ordering new airplanes, say Boeing has lost its nerve for aggressively developing bold new aircraft on its own. But according to the order books, Boeing has done its homework and built its widebodies right every time. Will they get the next one right? Only time will tell.

APPENDIX

Widebody Order Summary through December 2002

YEAR	747	767	777	DC-10	MD-11
1966	85				
1967	43				
1968	22			63	
1969	30			29	
1970	18			21	
1971	7			18	
1972	18			46	
1973	25			31	
1974	31			13	
1975	20			9	
1976	14			16	
1977	44			34	
1978	74	71		45	
1979	75	47		33	
1980	51	13		12	
1981	23	7		8	
1982	14	2		48	
1983	24	16		2	
1984	22	10		6	
1985	42	21		3	
1986	83	23		5	11
1987	65	57		2	20
1988	49	82		2	44
1989	56	96			18
1990	124	53	49		37
1991	32	67	25		10
1992	23	22	40		7
1993	2	53	20		6
1994	16	17			4
1995	33	22	88		9
1996	61	44	78		10
1997	36	80	55		11
1998	14	37	65		13
1999	35	29	21		
2000	27	9	116		
2001	16	45	30		
2002	17	8	32		
Totals	1371	931	619	446	200

Source: Boeing

INDEX

**Boeing 777:
The Technological Marvel**
ISBN 0-7603-0890-X

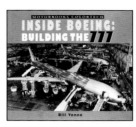

**Inside Boeing:
Building the 777**
ISBN 0-7603-1251-6

Boeing
ISBN 0-7603-0497-1

Classic American Airliners
ISBN 0-7603-0913-2

**Art of the Airways: A Poster
History of the World's Airlines**
ISBN 0-7603-1395-4

Air Force One
ISBN 0-7603-1055-6

Boeing Jetliner Databook
ISBN 0-7603-0928-0

**How to Draw Aircraft
Like a Pro**
ISBN 0-87938-0960-4

**America's Mighty
Eighth Air Force**
ISBN 0-9629-3596-4